IMPACT TECHNIQUES

for therapists

IMPACT TECHNIQUES

for therapists

Danie Beaulieu, Ph.D.

Translated from the French by Heidi S. Hoff

Routledge
Taylor & Francis Group
New York London

Routledge is an imprint of the
Taylor & Francis Group, an informa business

Published in 2006 by
Routledge
Taylor & Francis Group
270 Madison Avenue
New York, NY 10016

Published in Great Britain by
Routledge
Taylor & Francis Group
2 Park Square
Milton Park, Abingdon
Oxon OX14 4RN

Printed in the United States of America on acid-free paper
10 9 8 7 6 5 4 3 2 1

International Standard Book Number-10: 0-415-95389-8 (Softcover)
International Standard Book Number-13: 978-0-415-95389-4 (Softcover)
Library of Congress Card Number 2005029577

Library of Congress Cataloging-in-Publication Data

Beaulieu, Danie, 1961-
[Techniques d'impact. English]
Impact techniques for therapists / Danie Beaulieu ; translated from the French by Heidi S. Hoff.
p. cm.
Includes bibliographical references and index.
ISBN 0-415-95389-8 (pb : alk. paper)
1. Psychotherapy. I. Title.

RC480.B324 2006
616.89--dc22   2005029577

Taylor & Francis Group is the Academic Division of Informa plc.

Visit the Taylor & Francis Web site at
http://www.taylorandfrancis.com

and the Routledge Web site at
http://www.routledge-ny.com

I warmly dedicate this book to all my colleagues who share my passion for helping people fully become themselves.

Contents

CHAPTER 1

Impact Techniques Using Objects and Props 1

Preface

What are Impact Techniques? One answer is: they are techniques stemming from Impact Therapy, an approach developed by Edward Jacobs, Ph.D., professor of counseling psychology and rehabilitation at West Virginia University. Impact Therapy is distinct in its eclectic approach and its synergistic integration of many contemporary models of psychotherapeutic intervention, particularly Ericksonian hypnosis, solution-oriented psychotherapy, Reality Therapy, Neurolinguistic Programming, Rational Emotive Behavioral Therapy, Transactional Analysis, Gestalt, and, recently, Proaction Theory.

Another way of describing Impact Techniques would simply be to say that they are techniques with a lot of Impact because they permit clients to record more rapidly and remember longer the important messages transmitted during a therapy session. Why? Because Impact Techniques respect mnemonic laws, in other words, the principles whose application permits our memory systems to easily and permanently assimilate information. This is what most particularly characterizes Impact Therapy: the use of mnemotechniques—techniques and tricks that enhance the creation and retention of new memories—that notably make use of multisensory communication to translate messages into the various languages of the body. It is a question of talking not only to the client's ears, but also to their eyes, body, and all the human sensory modalities. Memory contains much more than just words, which becomes particularly significant when treating children or any client with a limited aptitude for verbal expression.

These mnemonic laws have been the subject of many studies, research projects, and articles, but for some inexplicable reason—unless we can blame Freud or Rogers and their praise for therapeutic neutrality—they have never been put to good use in psychotherapy. In fact, the people who use this avant-garde knowledge are mostly marketing experts—and they use it to sell hamburgers, cigarettes, and beer! They understand how memory functions better than do most psychotherapists. By way of proof, you just have to look at the results they obtain from 30-second commercials that are shown just a few times! They can adroitly modify consumer behavior without the consumer even noticing and without encountering resistance. We may not agree with the means they use to attain their ends, but we cannot deny their effectiveness. These specialists possess knowledge that every therapist should master. These same mnemonic tools can add enormously to the impact of the helping process, in less time, while permitting us to reach people who do not respond to the conventional methods of "talk therapy," that is, approaches based solely on verbal modalities.

My objective in this book is to provide you with knowledge of mnemotechniques that can be integrated into your work and to offer you a host of Impact Techniques you can use with your clients—no matter which approach you currently favor. My hope is that, using these techniques, you will find a justification for the creativity that you already bring to each intervention, discover new ways of working with your clients, and experience a surge of renewed energy and enthusiasm for helping your clients.

Good reading!

Danie Beaulieu, Ph.D.

Introduction

Fundamentals of Impact Techniques

When I use or present Impact Techniques, I always get some remarkable reactions. People are always surprised to feel so much impact from such simple objects and experiences. But nothing is surprising about it when we understand how the brain and memory function. The following section presents the eight major mnemotechnique principles whose application favor the creation of more rapid and stronger memory imprints when working with your clients, as well as examples of their use in psychotherapy.

Mnemotechnique Principle #1:
Take Multisensory Learning into Account

Human beings learn from the totality of their senses, not only with their ears, the sense that psychotherapy tends to depend on most, if not exclusively. In fact, the "audio system" is one of the least important sensory modalites in neuropsychological terms and one of the least reliable. Have you ever spoken to a client and become conscious that, not only was he not listening to you, but he was recording some other information entirely while you were doing your utmost to help him? This type of failed impact greatly affects the morale of the helping professional and the quality of the therapist–client relationship, as well as leading to a certain demotivation for both parties. We often turn to the well-known response: "Well, he just wasn't ready" or "I tried everything," which really means, "I said everything I could say. He doesn't understand, so I can't do anything else for him."

Fortunately, other sensory systems can be used to reach people and often they are much more efficient. Among these we find notably the "video system": the eyes. Did you know that studies of human neurophysiology have estimated that 60% of the information that flows to the brain comes via the eyes? How many of us have learned to talk to our clients' eyes? Think about it: Are radio commercials more or less effective than television commercials? Why? The answer is clear: if we talk to the eyes in addition to recruiting the verbal centers of the brain, we greatly increase the effect we can have on the person receiving the message. For the Impact therapist, the essential question is not "How can I say this to my client?" but rather "How can I show him or make him experience this?"

These postulates have been the subject of scientific research. It has been demonstrated many times that the cortical responses in the auditory and visual areas of the brain increase more when a subject is exposed to a bimodal sensorial stimulus compared to the total of the responses to separate unimodal visual and auditory stimuli. In other words, more neurons are activated when a message combines both visual and verbal elements compared to the sum of the activity provoked when each of these modalities is stimulated separately (Calvert, 2001; Calvert, Brammer, Bullmore, et al., 1999; Calvert, Campbell, & Brammer, 2000; Calvert, Hansen, Iversen, et al., 2001). In addition, adding a visual component to a message engages some regions of the brain involved in memory functions more rapidly and automatically (Grady, McIntosh, Rajah, et al., 1997).

Let's look at an example of this multisensory principle as it applies to psychotherapy.

You are meeting with a young man who has everything he needs to succeed in school but who fails because he doesn't apply himself. Young people can easily tell when an adult is about to give them a moral lesson: before the first word is even spoken, the child has already turned off his "headphones." We have all been there, haven't we? In contrast, every child is interested by an unexpected surprise. To foil his resistance, recruit his other senses and create a visual and kinesthetic experience. Place several plastic cups on the table to represent different "departments" of his life (e.g., skateboarding, Internet, friends, TV, video games) and save the last one for school. Already, you have generated a new response in the boy: instead of being on the defensive, he is interested and trying to understand the reason for this bit of staging. Involve him physically by giving him a cup filled with water. Explain to him that the water represents all the energy he has and ask him to distribute the water in the plastic cups to show you where he invested his energy during the past week. Did he go skateboarding, surf the Internet, play with friends, watch television? The boy should pour water into each of the cups to show the amount of time he devoted to each activity. Since the cup for school is placed last in the row, chances are that he will not have much water left for that aspect of his life. As there is a direct proportional relationship between our investment and the results we obtain, it is easy to *see* why school is not going so well. You can certainly *say* the same things to the boy, but if his eyes have not understood the message, it usually will not be recorded with as much impact. Guillemette Isnard, the French neurophysiologist, affirms that "information is integrated when all the senses have had their say" (Isnard, 1990, p. 79). The young man now has three keys to retrieve the information: the verbal key, the visual key, and the kinesthetic key. These three senses will work synergistically to repeat the same message. By involving more neurons, we amplify our intervention. It is like trying to push a very heavy weight: it is much easier for three people working together to make it move than for one person working alone.

Note that, by creating a little scene with such staging, you create the possibility of continuing to explore the metaphor and "seeding" solutions. For example, you can pour the water back into the original cup and ask the boy to show you what he should do if he wants to do better in school. At once, his body is engaged in creating that possibility and in creating his new version. It does not matter whether the verbal modality resists, the body will have already recorded the information. In the following sessions, you can revisit this experience and thus radically reduce the warm-up period that occurs at the beginning of every session. The cups can become your assessment tool to evaluate the actions taken during the previous week. Where did the client invest his energy during that time? Did he get the results he was hoping for?

Impact Techniques are also very flexible. The technique in the preceding example could also work well with young people who do not invest themselves in their friendships or extracurricular activities (or the opposite), and with those who invest too much energy in their failures, their parents' divorce, or in self-denigration. This technique could also suit adults, to help them reflect on the investment they make in various aspects of daily life.

When creating such an experience, only a few words are necessary. The information is illustrated, recorded, and integrated in a novel way, without being reshaped by the verbal thought process.

Children are among those who have the most difficulty with words, not only when learning them, but also when using them to express their feelings. In contrast, their spontaneity and their transparence are fully put to good use with the Impact approach. They feel naturally competent and at ease in a situation in which implicit language is used to communicate. Adults and adolescents are equally attracted by the simplicity, efficacy, and concrete aspect of this approach. In addition, they feel smart because they grasp the message and integrate it rapidly. All these elements favor not only better use of memory systems, but also increased motivation and improvement of the therapeutic relationship.

That does not mean that we should abandon the verbal modality. For one thing, that would be practically impossible in the context of psychotherapy and, for another, the use of words can most certainly add to the process. Words really do possess enormous power. The ad men at McDonald's know this well. Have you ever heard a competitor's name mentioned in their ads or heard them talk about microwaves, fatty meals, or frozen foods? Of course not. Instead, they choose words that attract, that create desire in consumers, and that are congruent with their projected values. They use words that interest and engage the potential customer, like "delicious," "fresh," "fast," suggesting that it is the perfect place for a family outing with the kids.

In an experiment on the power of words, photos of two beautiful women were presented to a group of volunteers, who were then asked which of the two women they found the prettiest. In the first vote, the group split about 50:50. Then, the same experiment was conducted with a fresh group of subjects, but they were told that the name of the first woman was Jennifer and that of the second woman was Gertrude. The first woman received 80% of the votes (Kotler,

2003). Words, like the names in that experiment, can push buttons on our inner control boards, activating the circuits of related past experiences. Each word activates the neural circuits that are specific to that word, with all their sensory and affective content. For therapeutic purposes, it is a question of knowing how to wake up the networks that will help our clients generate the desired thoughts and actions. This realization gives one pause when therapists so commonly ask questions such as "Do you feel depressed? Have you been thinking about suicide?" Similarly, questions such as "What is the problem?" lead the client to focus on what is not going well. In contrast, if you ask "What changes do you want to make in your life currently?" or "What would you like to improve in your life?", this allows clients to pay attention to what they would like to add to their lives and to become proactive in making progress toward their own goals.

It is also clear that words expressing metaphors make the right hemisphere of the brain become more involved, in contrast to purely explicit language that recruits primarily the left hemisphere (Bottini, Corcoran, Sterzi, et al., 1994; Brownell, Simpson, Bihrle, et al., 1990; Faust & Weisper, 2000). This information is important when we consider that "the activation or creation of connections between thousands of neurons will always increase the performance of the brain, never diminish it. This cannot but establish privileged communication between our sense organs and our cortical areas, and as a result, alter the interpretation, the perception that we have of the exterior world" (Isnard, 1990).

Thus, the verbal modality can have a remarkable impact on memory if one knows how to exploit its full potential.

Mnemotechnique Principle #2: Make Abstract Concepts Concrete

What do these three ads have in common? Toilet paper linked to the softness of kittens; an insurance company using an elephant as a logo to represent its strength, longevity, and size; and an appliance manufacturer using a bored repairman to illustrate the reliability of its equipment? The common denominator is that each offers the consumer a concrete symbol to incarnate the abstract qualities of their product or service. Why would they do that? It's simple: the brain retains concrete information more easily than it does abstract ideas. Why not take this into account in the process of helping our clients?

For example, when my son Jordane was 9 years old, his third-grade teacher placed a great deal of emphasis on the value of solidarity. She gave a lot of importance to collaboration and mutual respect: it was at the heart of her teaching approach. After attending a parent-teacher meeting at the beginning of the year, during which she told us about her teaching philosophy, I returned home and asked Jordane if he knew what "solidarity" meant, since I knew that this was probably a new word for him. He answered very seriously, "It's real important to Mrs. Forest." I repeated, "But do you know what it means?" I got the same answer again. Clearly, he had recorded with his body and eyes the degree to which this principle was important to his teacher, but he was completely ignorant of what it really involved. In fact, in pursuing my inquiry, I realized that he had created a definition based on what he already knew, that is the word "solid." So every time Mrs. Forest talked about solidarity, my son showed his solidarity by becoming "solid" and rigid as an iron rod. Not the best conditions for learning.

Having detected that many of her students did not seem to understand what she wanted so much to teach them (I was relieved to learn that my son was not the only one in his class in that situation), his teacher asked me to create an Impact Technique that could help her students to understand her message. I suggested that she buy a 30-piece jigsaw puzzle and give one piece to each of the students (there were 26 in the class) and to distribute the remaining four pieces to herself and the three teaching aids. Children are very familiar with puzzles and associate them with pleasure, play, and the idea "I can do this." They also know that each piece is different, each has its proper place, and all the pieces must be assembled to yield a complete and satisfying result. A perfect analogy to illustrate the role of each child in the class: each should contribute their own "piece" (even the shyest children will understand the importance of sharing their opinion) and respect others' "pieces" (that is, their ideas and personality) because they are part of the whole "class puzzle."

This metaphor also helps children recognize that there are different styles and shapes of pieces in the puzzle: "corner pieces," who may prefer to be calm, without too many people around them; and "center pieces," who like being in the thick of things, who are always raising their hand, ready to answer the teacher's questions, and who have lots of friends. Then there are the "edge pieces" who adapt well to the needs of others—they are calm when they are near "corner pieces" and can be very active when they are with friends who have a more "center" style. To make a rapid and accurate assessment of a group at the beginning of the year, the teacher can offer a puzzle piece to each student and ask them to work together to assemble their pieces. As the body cannot lie, the teacher will rapidly see which students are "center pieces" (the first to dive into the game), "edge pieces" (who are alert, watchful, and ready to give their piece to a "center" student so that he or she can put it in the puzzle), and "corner pieces" (who remain in their seats or far from the group until things have calmed down around the table).

The exercise is so concrete that the students absorb the message while having fun, and recollection of its lessons is that much more powerful because the learning experience was based on coenesthesis, that is, general sensorial awareness. In the future, when dealing with a student who is overly assertive, the teacher just has to say, "Charles, have you already put in your piece today? Yes? Well then, it might be better to let others put theirs in, too." At once the child remembers the images and sensations that remind him of the importance of thinking about the whole group and not just about his own personal benefit.

By the way, this would be a great exercise to do with any group, be it a group of coworkers or a therapy group.

Another puzzle exercise is outstanding for making the notion of parental separation concrete for a child. Give the child two pieces of the same puzzle that are not contiguous (or of two different puzzles, if you think that suits the situation better). Ask the child to put them together. After a little while, he will realize that it is impossible to do so. Then ask him which one of the pieces is wrong, which one should change. Clearly, the two are what they are, they simply do not go together. If you take the time to write the name of each parent on back of one of the puzzle pieces, this will be enough to help the child understand that his parents cannot and should not persist in trying to stay together. They each have their place somewhere, but they need to look for the other pieces. By making the explanation very concrete, superfluous discussions are avoided. The child also understands that he is not responsible for the fact that the two pieces do not fit. If you wish, carefully choose the pieces you use so that the child is represented by a piece that fits with both parental pieces.

Mnemotechnique Principle #3: Build on What Is Already Known

Do you think an Italian would have an easier time learning Spanish or German? Why? Clearly Spanish, because it is more similar to his native language. Would a doctor have more or less difficulty than a photographer learning to become a pharmacist? Naturally, the doctor would have an advantage because he already knows a lot about the health field. Despite our best efforts to make psychology accessible to all, the concepts of neurosis, defense mechanisms, projection, and superego are often nothing but obscure and strange terms for most of our clients, especially the younger ones. When you create an experience based on what is already known, as in the case of the jigsaw puzzle, you implicitly reawaken a host of cognitive, emotional, visual, and kinesthetic reactions—sometimes without the client even realizing it. All these connections create an opening and consequently better assimilation of the message you wanted to transmit. Most Westerners are much more inclined to enjoy a good meal using a fork than with chopsticks; just as chopsticks make many of us a bit awkward, psychotherapy that does not respect the client's memory baggage may provoke a bit of hesitation.

Thus, one constant concern for the Impact therapist is to draw on the client's memory archives to create connections, consolidate the relationship, overcome resistance, provoke significant reflections, and create anchors that allow the internal process to continue beyond the end of the session.

Let's examine an example of the application of this principle within the framework of a therapeutic relationship. When working with a client who refuses to talk about prior difficult experiences (trauma; sexual, physical or psychological abuse; harassment, etc.), use a garbage-filled trash bag closed with several knots. Allow the client to examine the bag and to notice the odors it emits. Then pose a series of questions, such as: "Do you think that by keeping the bag closed, the odor of the garbage will increase or decrease over time? Do you have a bag like this inside you, that contains bad memories? Are there many bad memories in it? Have you noticed that, since you have been carrying that bag around, the people who've known you for a long time say that you're not quite the same and sense that you're not happy?" You can easily devote an entire session, or more, to developing this analogy. Clients, especially young clients, often do not understand what a diagnosis of post-traumatic stress disorder means, but they certainly understand garbage. By using their knowledge base (their expertise) you help them to understand themselves better and to realize the importance of emptying their trash bag.

This principle resembles Milton Erickson's concept of "utilization." Erickson advocated utilizing the client's words and habitual activities and applying them in a new way to facilitate the client–therapist relationship, reduce resistance, and enrich the therapeutic process. In Impact Therapy, we "utilize" familiar objects to attain the same goals.

Mnemotechnique Principle #4:
Stimulate the Emotions

Memory is directly related to emotions. Do you remember where you were on September 11, 2001 when you learned about the terrorist attack in New York? Some events, like the birth of a child, the death of a loved one, or an important graduation, are permanently etched in our neurologic networks because they are associated with strong feelings. Not only do strong emotions ensure the rapid recording of the information, but also its durability.

There are a number of ways of applying this principle in psychotherapy. First, as has already been mentioned, if you use an object familiar to your client and you know that the object is already highly emotionally charged, the efficacy of your intervention will benefit from a significant short cut. For example, you can place on a chair a case of beer to represent the alcoholism of a parent or a box of candies to represent a pedophile and his favorite strategy for luring his victim to him. Similarly, a child's favorite pencil can symbolize his willingness to apply himself to his school work and a photo of a happy family event can help reestablish contact with the bright side of life, despite current difficulties. Everyone has certain objects associated with a strong emotional charge.

You can also ask the client to identify an object that can translate what he is feeling. In so doing, he will be forced to examine his deepest emotions and internal images, and he will need to invest his body and soul in the exercise. When working with a client who had had a leg amputated at a level that made it impossible to wear a prosthesis, I asked him to choose an object that described his new condition. He selected an empty beer bottle, which he turned upside down so that it balanced unsteadily on its narrow neck. This simple representation had the power to bring him to tears: in it he saw himself, balanced precariously on one leg, vulnerable to the smallest external pressure. A long and rich exploration of his feelings followed.

Symbols are very powerful because they can translate a thousand words, thoughts, feelings, and emotions into a single element. If you do not feel inspired, allow your clients to find their own symbol and you will be surprised at the rapidity with which you can reach the heart of the matter. Or you can meet your client halfway by giving him an object that he can shape or manipulate to translate his reality. For example, when working with a 7-year-old boy, you can offer him Monopoly money or playing cards and ask him to quantify some of his behaviors using symbols. Was hitting his friend like an ace of hearts or a three of spades? Was it like $1 or $100 or maybe $500? If you explain the exercise well, the session becomes a game and you will learn a lot about your young client. Are you starting to think that such a session might have more impact than simply talking about those behaviors? It is bound to, because you are following at least four of the mnemotechnique principles describe here.

There are at least two other ways of engaging the emotions during the therapeutic process. The first is to dramatize the situation, to amplify the problem. For example, if the client is obsessed with a certain situation (the divorce of parents, drug use, a handicap, failure in school, end of a romantic relationship, etc.), write the name of the object of the obsession on a piece of cardboard (such as backing for a pad of paper because it is associated with something common and ordinary that is thrown out when no longer useful). Then, ask the client to hold it very close to her face—ideally just an inch or so from her nose—using both hands so that she sees nothing but the word on the cardboard. Next, offer her a series of tempting things, which she evidently will not be able to see because the cardboard is in front of her eyes. Soon enough, the client will start feeling frustrated at being deprived of all the things she does not have access to by "holding" her attention solely on her obsession. The more you lead the client to distance herself from the cardboard, by suggesting that she gradually move it away from her eyes, the more she will feel relieved by the simple fact that her vision is no longer restricted and she can breathe more easily. It then becomes a simple task to link that same feeling of relief, on a psychological level, with choosing to distance herself from the object of her obsession. The impact in these cases comes not only from feeling the emotion of frustration, but also from the surprise generated by the experience itself.

The other way to engage the client's emotions is to create codes. Let me explain. Our brain reacts in a special way to codes. The human being is a creature of habit, as has been emphasized by Hyrum Smith, the designer of the popular Franklin Day Planner. He estimates that 95% of our reactions have become automatic as a result of our previous experiences (Smith, 1996). This means that some stimuli can provoke predictable reactions. For example, have you created a loving code with your spouse, a little word like "dear," "love," "sweetie," or "honey"? Or perhaps you have such a code with your child, pet, coworker, or sibling. Given that the use of such codes is associated in your mind with close relationships, anyone who uses this type of code with you, using the same tone of voice, can create a sense of closeness with you spontaneously—or at least much more quickly than without using this automatism. Don't believe it? It is normal to doubt it—because most of the time these reactions are completely automatic. You are not even aware that it is happening.

Try to think of a stranger who called you by a nice nickname in a tone of voice that seemed sincere. Didn't you establish a friendly rapport with that person more rapidly? Codes sometimes make us react in strange ways. Here is another example. My brother-in-law is a policeman. We were driving together when he was stopped for speeding. The officer who came to the window to ask for his driver's license and car registration did not know my brother-in-law from Adam, but they had a code: both were wearing a badge. As soon as my brother-in-law presented his badge, they become instant friends, and he did not get a ticket because they shared a code.

Another example. Every spring break, I take a trip to Cuba with my son. Last year, while I was talking with Jordane on the beach, someone interrupted our conversation. "Hey! Bonjour! Are you from Quebec?" a stranger called out in a tone of great familiarity. He had detected a code: we had been speaking in Quebecois French in a Spanish-speaking area. This man would never have thought of talking to us if we had all been on our home turf, but hearing his own language on a Cuban beach made him suddenly feel very friendly. Once again, it was the code we shared that created a sense of closeness.

In therapy, every time you use an object or a bit of staging, it becomes a form of code between you and your client. Use it often. Instead of telling a shy child to share his point of view, ask him if he has added his "puzzle piece" today. As your client is leaving, give him a plastic cup to remind him of the session and of the importance of investing in the right department of his life during the week. Use and reuse the codes that you have created during your meetings. Each time you do so, the code will reinforce the message that, "We share a unique language that no one else can understand; we are thus accomplices in this therapy and share a special closeness."

Mnemotechnique Principle #5:
Arouse Interest

Can you remember your neighbor's license plate number? Do you know the color and style of the building number displayed on the financial institution you use most often? Do you remember whether the cashier at the grocery store wears a ring? Exactly what does the cover of the menu look like at your favorite restaurant? Surprisingly, it is difficult to answer most of these questions. You have been exposed to these things dozens, if not thousands, of times. Your eyes have seen them, but your brain has not retained the information—because they were not of interest. Memory functions on the basis of interest.

Contrary to what one might think, our clients are not always "interested" in talking—or hearing—about themselves, their problems, and possible solutions. Part of our work consists of completely involving our clients in the therapeutic process, and this requires making that process more interesting. Generating interest often means creating surprise, the unexpected, or working with elements that give rise to desire or pleasure. Every time you create a novel experience, you generate interest. In fact, you activate two spontaneous reactions. The first is the response of the brain that attempts to complete an incomplete data set, to "fill in the blanks." It is another automatism. Thus, when you introduce elements that seem out of context in your discussion, your client will try to understand why you are doing so, and his attitude will change from unengaged to curious. The second reaction is the recruitment of "uncontaminated circuits" that allow you to overcome resistance. In other words, when you directly approach a problem verbally with a client who does not want to hear about it, you are facing major opposition. In contrast, if you approach the client by suggesting a card game or asking him to look at a piece of paper that you have torn apart, you can catch him off-balance and entice him to follow you rather than distance himself from you. Once you have gotten his attention, your message will be etched much more easily and permanently.

For example, if an involuntary adolescent client knows that he must come see you because his parents or his school have found out that he has been using drugs, he may show substantial resistance to any and all discussion of the subject—he is simply not interested in what you have to say. But if you approach him with a coin, say a quarter, and ask him to take it, you activate strong new neurological circuits—everyone is interested in money—while using surprise and pleasure, and mobilizing all his senses and the corresponding neurons. When the adolescent tries to take the coin, you simply tell him, "No, just the 25! Take just the numbers 2 and 5 on the quarter." Surprise again! Something interesting! It is impossible to take just the numbers off a coin. At that point, you have an opportunity to send your message: "You see, this is kind of like taking drugs. You can't have just the pleasure of taking them. The pleasure comes with all the rest—the money problems, your parents on your back, problems at school, having to hide what you're doing. Every time you see a quarter, think of that." Even if the adolescent did not want to start a discussion of the subject, you have at least succeeded in creating a significant anchor that will continue to work in his mind, whether he comes back to your office or not, because you know that he will see quarters in the future, and often. Do you think there is a good chance that your client will remember this experience after leaving your office? Even if, intellectually, he tries to ridicule your intervention, his eyes and his body will repeat your message to him, whether he is conscious of it.

Milton Erickson frequently exploited the principle of arousing interest. In a well-known case, he recounted how he helped a little girl who resented everyone because her nickname was Freckles, a reference to the abundance of them on her face (Rosen, 1991). The little girl was very resistant to the idea of meeting with Dr. Erickson. As she entered his office, before she had a chance to say a word, he yelled, "You're a thief! You stole!" Instead of approaching the subject of her freckles directly, knowing the associated resistances, he created an experience to displace the debate. In so doing, he forced the girl to take interest: she had to defend herself and her reputation. Also note that this intervention aroused the client's emotions tremendously. She was furious at being gratuitously accused like that. "I'm not a thief! I've never stolen anything!" she cried. "Yes, you are a thief. You stole something and I even know what you stole," Erickson replied. "You have no proof. You couldn't have: I haven't stolen anything!" she retorted. Erickson persisted, "I even know where you were when you stole it." The girl was really very angry, but she was also "interested" in defending her reputation, so she continued to listen to Erickson as he said, "I'm going to tell you what you stole and where you were. You were in the kitchen setting the table. You stretched up high on a shelf to reach the cookie jar your mother had put the cinnamon rolls in and you ended up with cinnamon all over your face. Your face is full of cinnamon!" Since the girl was so excited, intense, and eager to receive information, this reframing completely transformed the rage she felt about her freckles. Now she had a cinnamon face—and she loved cinnamon rolls!

Dr. Erickson spontaneously applied many of the mnemotechnique principles: he made his interventions interesting, aroused emotions, used information already known to the client, and got the visual sense and the body involved in very concrete ways.

Mnemotechnique Principle #6: Add Pleasure to Your Interventions

How many commercials use humor or appeal to the idea of pleasure? I do not have the answer because statistics on the subject are impossible to find given that commercials change constantly, but casual observation suggests that the proportion is very high. Just a brief look around is enough: breweries often link their product to meetings among friends; jeans manufacturers associate their products with sex (sex is very popular for advertising many products!); McDonald's gives the illusion of making your family happy and united on every visit; producers of detergent show your clothes whiter than white in the blink of an eye, and so on. In short, advertisers all try to awaken some type of pleasure response in consumers and to link that response to their products.

The fact is that people understand the importance of the pleasure principle: they are attracted to pleasure, they seek it, and they constantly return to it. Suppose your circle of acquaintances includes some people you have a lot of fun with, who always amuse you, and others whose conversations always end up being a long series of complaints about everything imaginable. Who are you more likely to invite when organizing an evening among friends? Who do you think of when planning a fun weekend trip?

Do you favor a certain type of pen, a particular variety of wine, a brand of detergent? These products have all given you pleasure and so you are faithful to them and seek them out again.

There is an important lesson in all of this for therapists, parents, and romantic partners: we need to ask ourselves what awakens pleasure in the other person and use those pathways to transmit our messages.

Suppose you are working on politeness and respect for others with an adolescent boy. Those two words—politeness and respect—are not too popular among young people, so it is just as well to avoid saying them, much less repeating them, at the risk of obtaining the opposite result to the one hoped for. How can you approach the subject in an interesting way and avoid provoking hostile reactions? One suggestion would be to show him a gift bag, saying that you have something special to offer him. Who doesn't feel immense pleasure at the thought of receiving a surprise? Then give him a choice between your gift bag and an obviously soiled facial tissue. Do not hesitate to use it to blow your nose in front of him. Make the process spectacular, with bugle sounds and all. Then ask him to choose which of the two he prefers: the gift bag or the very used tissue. The first response is usually a burst of laughter. Great! We have just achieved our objective of incorporating pleasure in the intervention. The client's second response is clearly to choose the gift bag. But why? The tissue could easily be hiding a gold nugget, and the gift bag might be completely empty, or worse, filled with used tissues! Nonetheless, everyone chooses the gift bag…because of the packaging. Ask the boy how he "packages" the messages he wants to transmit. Have his most recent conversations resembled a used tissue paper or a nicely wrapped present? Do his words inspire the desire to accept or to avoid what he is offering? Using this technique, the boy can understand that he needs to learn how to phrase his comments to others if he wants to be heard and, above all, if he wants to be understood.

Since this is not a miracle method, you will clearly need to repeat these lessons in politeness, but instead of doing so verbally, you can simply show him the gift bag with a small smile and a wink. By the way, avoid taking out the used tissue again. It is important to expose the client to the message you want to develop, not the contrary. Do Burger King's ads talk about McDonald's? Of course not. They do not want you to even think about the competition. The same thing applies in your work. Once you have established its meaning, use only the positive symbol that is associated with the behavior you want to reinforce.

When working with a client who is exhausted but refuses to stop working or even to slow down, you could hold a toothpick up vertically and ask him to place a heavy book, or even a brick, on top of it. The result will clearly be that the toothpick will break under the weight of the book. You would get the same result with a popsicle stick. What would happen if you used a pencil or a nail? Ask your client which of those objects is the best analogy for his current state. Is he more like a toothpick or a nail? Is he taking on a weight of responsibility that is within his strength? This example will elicit a more pleasant response than centering the discussion entirely on his fatigue and his weakness. This type of intervention engages the client's resources and facilitates the process.

Mnemotechnique Principle #7: Simplicity Is...More Simple

Leonardo da Vinci said, "Simplicity is the ultimate sophistication." It is certainly the royal road to helping our clients assimilate new information and feel at home in the therapeutic process. For example, which of each of the following pairs of sentences is the easiest to remember?

Visible vapors that issue from carbonaceous materials
are a harbinger of imminent conflagration.

OR

Where there's smoke, there's fire.
We utilized a concert of cross-functional expertise.

OR

People from different departments talked to each other.
Don't impact employee incentivization programs.

OR

Don't screw around with people's pay.

Did you choose? These examples are taken from Jack Trout and Steve Rivkin's 1998 book, *The Power of Simplicity*. The authors emphasize not only the power, but also the rarity, of simplicity. Many people avoid simplicity. The authors affirm that, in general, companies will pay more for a "complicated" seminar—that no one understands a word of—than they will for a simple training session that their employees can quickly integrate and put into practice. Not very logical, but very real.

Many therapists are hesitant to use Impact Techniques that require the use of modeling clay, balloons, and rubber bands because they think that these props are not very serious, not very "professional." However, John Sculley, former CEO of Apple Computer, adopted da Vinci's position as a guiding design principle for the company: "Simplicity is the ultimate in sophistication." Nonetheless, it seems that this principle is easily forgotten. Keep it simple and your clients—old and young alike, those who are highly educated and those trained in the school of life—will quickly feel at ease with you. People remember information more easily when it is expressed in simple terms—it's as simple as that!

For example, one of my clients, who also happened to be an amputee, seemed to be completely disconnected from reality. He did not respond or barely responded to questions. Three weeks earlier, this 19-year-old had had both his legs amputated very close to the hip after a car accident. The doctors were not sure whether they could save his right arm. The other therapists who had worked with the young man to offer him psychological support all used the same metaphor to describe his state: "He's floating." When an Impact therapist hears metaphoric language, she immediately tries to translate the experience into concrete terms.

When I approached his bed in the hospital room, I said nothing at all. I wanted to provoke his curiosity, his interest, a desire to understand why I was there and why I was doing what I was doing. I wanted him to come to me, rather than to impose a relationship on him. I took a pitcher from the shelf by his bed and poured some water into a glass next to it, without explanation. He watched me with a somewhat interested air, as if wondering, "Is that for me or for you?" By way of answer, I tore off a scrap of paper from my pad (we have to make do with what we find at hand) and took my time crumpling it into a little ball that I then placed on the surface of the water so that it floated.

The client's body reacted immediately: his sadness surged to the surface and tears started running down his cheeks. We still had not said a word. Then he said, showing that he had identified with the floating paper, "I don't want it to sink." Wow! I had goosebumps! I had tears in my eyes, too. We were together as witnesses sharing the experience, rather than separately as a psychologist and her traumatized patient, whose resistance needs to be overcome.

I started touching the ball of paper, making it move from one side to the other in the glass. Then I asked him, "What could make it sink?" He said without hesitation, "I can't wear a prosthesis." The doctors were uncertain on this score because the amputations had been made close to the pelvis. "If you can't wear a prosthesis, you think that will make it sink?" I said, and, while the client's attention was still very focused on the glass, I started pushing the paper down in the water with my finger. As soon as the paper disappeared under the water, the client's face reddened and he said quickly, "It won't sink that far." It was a magic moment, both of us immobilized in a sort of trance, which happens fairly regularly in visual and kinesthetic interventions.

Before leaving the patient, I mentioned that I was only in the hospital that day by chance, to give a workshop to a group of therapists. He suggested that I come to visit him the next time I was in the area. However, while we were verbally occupied with that conversation, I was also sending another message by lifting the ball of paper out of the water—nonverbally suggesting that he would not "sink" and that he would pull through. Three weeks later I visited him again at the hospital. As soon as he saw me enter the room, he reached over to take something out of the drawer beside the bed. It was the ball of paper that I had left with him. With tears in his eyes, he said, "It didn't sink. The doctors told me that I'd be able to wear prostheses and keep my right arm." Neither of us was able to continue talking, so we just stayed there for a few minutes, very moved, his hand in mine, contemplating that little scrap of paper. Personally, I have found that simplicity leads more directly and rapidly to my clients' hearts and, consequently, forms a much deeper and longer lasting connection, no matter their age or the problems they are facing.

Mnemotechnique Principle #8:
Repeat, Repeat…Without Having to Repeat

Most of what we learn has to be repeated many times before all our senses can master it, unless a very potent emotion is involved. For example, if you burn yourself while cooking, you generally do not have to repeat that experience to understand the danger associated with hot stoves. On the other hand, it is practically impossible to learn a foreign language or ride a bicycle after a single try: repetition is needed. In the same way, when a client wants to modify a behavior that has gone on for years, repetition will be needed to make the desired change.

However, repetition can easily become boring, as much for the person who has to do it as for the teacher, coach, or therapist who is making them do it. With Impact Techniques, it is possible to repeat without repeating. Here's how.

The fact that tangible elements are used in the Impact approach provides a major advantage: the simple props we use remain visually available, especially if we take pains to choose something that clients normally find in daily life. These props thus continue to function as reminders of the discussion of the client's problem, long after she has left the therapist's office. When your contact with a client is limited to 1 hour per week, you only have 60 minutes to influence her, her perceptions, and the behavior she wants to modify. On the other hand, if you create an anchoring link between a familiar object and your message, every time your client sees that object—often many times per week—she will have the benefit of a repetition of the concepts discussed with you and the impact of your intervention will be increased that much more. You do not even have to be present for the information to be repeated: the objects that you used during the session will transmit the message for you several times a day, and do so using the major sensory pathways of the brain—the visual and the kinesthetic.

In your own life, have you ever held onto an object of no monetary value (e.g., a rock, postcard, piece of driftwood collected on a walk with someone dear to you) simply because you intuitively felt that it would serve as your return ticket to the emotions you felt when you acquired it? The ability of an object of no apparent value to awaken echoes of memory and emotion should not be underestimated. The objects that you give to your clients to take with them after a session (cards, cups, puzzle pieces, etc.) will not only help them continue to reflect on your discussion, but they are also a very effective way to create a relationship that unites client and therapist.

Impact Techniques: More than Simply Mnemotechniques

Although mnemotechniques constitute a major part of the Impact approach, there is much more to it than that.

Every time you use one of these techniques, you force the client to focus his attention on one thing, to center himself. Every minute becomes more profitable because both the client and the therapist are fully invested in the process.

What's more, the use of staging engages the client in action. Milton Erickson strongly believed in the need to put the client into action and to do so as rapidly as possible. He often asked his clients to hike up Squaw Peak, a local landmark near Phoenix, before coming to their first appointment. He wanted to force his clients to act, to do something concrete in order to see and feel the results. By using objects and creating experiences within the framework of the session, Impact Therapy sends an implicit yet clear message: you need to move, act, take action, and get physically and emotionally involved to get results.

Another advantage of this approach is that it interrupts the habitual reactions of the client. It is an ancient principle that if you always do the same thing you will invariably get the same results. To obtain different results, you need to do things differently. The techniques described in this introduction provide a new form of communication, reflection, and intervention based more on coenesthesis and feelings, rather than on logic and words. The client's usual patterns of functioning are interrupted, so that she experiences her situation through a concrete metaphor involving all her multiple intelligences. This generally leads to new perspectives that allow the client to develop a different vision and completely original solutions to the difficulties she is facing.

The client–therapist relationship is also very different in Impact Therapy. The two become observers of the objects and experiences presented. Instead of the client being on one side and the therapist on the other, the client and therapist are together in relation to the staging experience. Although experienced on the implicit level, this rapprochement is crucial in accelerating the creation of a bond of trust because the two protagonists are in the same camp.

Impact Techniques are universal and can be applied in many contexts with varied clienteles and problems. They also greatly decrease the resistance of the client because the problem is treated in an indirect way and because interest is immediately engaged by the proposed staging (when it is well adapted, naturally).

Finally, these tools add a lot of dynamism and energy to the process. Many therapists even say that this is the main advantage for them. They take greater pleasure in their work when using Impact Techniques. As the saying goes, whatever you enjoy doing, you tend to do well!

Impact Techniques
Using Objects and Props

CHAPTER 1

The use of visual tools makes therapy concrete and facilitates the concentration of the client on a specific theme. To this, two other advantages are added. The first is that the therapist always chooses visual objects regularly found in daily life. The fact that the client will see them again between sessions reinforces the benefits of the intervention. The second is that the objects are generally available and inexpensive. Consequently, the therapist can be equipped for a minimal cost, and even make a gift of one or another of the objects to clients, to encourage them to pursue their reflections after the session.

Sheet of Paper

A piece of paper can represent a relationship between two people. When smooth and clean, it symbolizes an agreeable and satisfying relationship; whereas when it is rumpled, torn or stained, it represents an unhealthy and harmful relationship.

Example 1

The Cost of Anger

A therapist is working with Charles, a client who has substantial difficulty with anger management. Charles says that he does not understand his wife's "excessive" reactions when he loses his temper.

Charles:

She knows very well that I'm not mean. I explode like that, but afterwards, it's over. It's always the same! She says she can't take it anymore and that if I don't change, she'll leave me.

Therapist:

If I understand you correctly, Charles, you blow off steam at Holly, saying a bunch of things that you don't really mean. Then you promptly forget them. But you don't understand why she doesn't forget them, too. Is that it?

Charles:

Yes, that's it!

Therapist:

Let's take a piece of paper. You see, it's nice and smooth and clean. Let's say that it represents your relationship with Holly, so I'll write "Charles and Holly" on it. (*The therapist writes the two names.*) What number, on a scale of 0 to 10, would you say expresses your attachment to this relationship?

Charles:

A 10, easily!

Therapist:

Now let's look at what happens when you are angry. (*The therapist imitates Charles when he loses his temper, based on the information provided by Charles, all the while vigorously crumpling the paper.*) "I told you to have supper ready at six because I've got a meeting! You're a total airhead! You know that it was important to me—you could've made an effort for once! What do I have to do to knock some sense into you?" (*The sheet of paper is completely crumpled and partially torn.*)

Charles:

(*Perplexed, he watches attentively.*)

Therapist:

(*Again playing the role of the client, the therapist tries to smooth out the sheet of paper as much as possible, while apologizing.*) "Oh, I'm sorry. I didn't mean to say that! You know that that meeting makes me nervous. Forget all that now. It's over!" (*The sheet of paper is still wrinkled despite the therapist's efforts to make it smooth again. Charles remains open mouthed, clearly touched by the analogy.*) What do you think of this demonstration, Charles?

Charles:

I understand much better why Holly reacts like she does, if she feels like that….

Therapist:

I have the impression that that's exactly what she's been trying to say to you for some time. You know, it's human to get angry; no matter how much we try to understand one another, I don't think we can completely avoid feeling angry sometimes. But it's very useful to learn how to manage those feelings in a healthy way. Would you be interested in trying?

Charles:

(*Convinced.*) Yes, absolutely!

Example 2
Relationship Assessment between a Girl and Her Father

A mother consults a therapist to get help for her 8-year-old daughter. The parents divorced 4 months ago and their shared custody of their only child has provoked a lot of confusion. The mother says that the father is violent and that, even if he has never yet hit the child, he would be capable of killing her. The gun collection that her ex-husband continues to enlarge worries her a lot. Because the mother has no proof to support her suspicions, the little girl is supposed to spend every other week at her father's home. After each visit, she comes back upset and the next week returns to her father's house with dread. Her anxiety, which seems to get worse with every visit, has gotten so bad that she has difficulty sleeping and concentrating in class. She has also developed many psychosomatic problems. In the following example, the therapist is alone with the child and is trying to determine if the facts as presented by the mother are correct or exaggerated.

Julie:

Papa is a little different. He can't do two things at the same time.

Therapist:

What do you mean?

Julie:

Like, when I get home from school, he can't talk to me because he says he has to cook. When we're at the table, he doesn't want to talk to me either because he says we're eating. And it's the same thing after dinner when we're clearing the table.

Therapist:

Okay, Julie. Let's say that this piece of paper represents your feelings when you are with your father. (*Slightly crumples one corner of the paper.*) Do you feel a little like that when you are at his house?

Julie:

Oh, no! When I go to his house, I feel like this! (*Julie takes the paper from the therapist's hands and crumples it completely.*) And when I get back to Mom's, I don't have time to calm down and smooth things out before I have to go back to Dad's already. (*The child is clearly frightened.*)

_____

This example clearly demonstrates how a simple piece of paper can help clarify the condition of a relationship.

Example 3
The "Secret" Paper

A third experience that can be created using paper consists of taking a piece of paper without saying a word and writing the word "secret" in the center while the client is watching. Then, the therapist asks the young client to fold the paper in half, then in quarters, then in eighths, and to keep folding it smaller and smaller.

Therapist:

That paper really reminds me of you. I think that you're a little like that piece of paper, all folded in on itself to hide a secret. I'd really like to help you with that secret, but because of the way you hide it, it's really difficult for me to find any way to help you. Do you think that you could open up that paper a little bit and share the secret with me?

(*Depending on the response of the client, and thanks to the concrete metaphor that the therapist has just created, many options are now available. You can ask the child to unfold the paper a little bit to represent how far he is willing to go in unveiling his secret to you. You can ask him what you could do to help him open the paper. Or, you can explore different aspects of the secret.*)

Have you had that secret for a long time? Has it always been so hidden? Did you promise someone never to tell? Is there someone you'd feel comfortable revealing the secret to?

❖ Modeling Clay

Modeling clay (such as Play-Doh) can be mixed, unmixed, and remodeled. It also has a sticky and adherent nature, like some kinds of memories and experiences. It proves to be very appropriate to illustrate many aspects of the therapeutic process.

Example 1

Those Who Want to Fix Everything in a Single Meeting, Despite Having Some Serious Problems

Gerald is 62 and has a painful and burdensome past. Despite a generally unsatisfactory existence, his immediate motivation for coming to therapy was to get help fixing a problem with his wife. According to Gerald, his wife opposes most of his plans, screams at him all day long, humiliates him, and accuses him over trivialities whenever she has the chance. For his part, the client says he submits silently. On the other hand, the client resists exploring his past and shares information about it in tiny bits and pieces. Despite this, the therapist is able to glean enough information to recognize the need to enlarge the agreed-upon scope of the intervention.

Therapist:

Gerald, here's my reading of your situation. (*The therapist takes out different colors of modeling clay and speaks with a gentle voice.*) You were placed in an orphanage when you were seven, while your brothers and sisters stayed in the family home. Are the feelings you had then similar to those you are describing to me to today, that you have with your wife? Are they the same feelings of rejection, of not being listened to, not having your needs met or your values respected? (*The client nods, half-agreeing, half-neutral, while the therapist picks up a ball of clay to illustrate the event.*)

And when you lost an eye in an accident and all the other boys and girls mocked you, would you say that the same feelings of rejection were hounding you? (*From the emotional, though discrete, reaction of the client, the therapist knows that he has touched a nerve. So he adds another color to the ball of modeling clay, which he blends in with the previous one.*)

When you were fired from your job despite all your accomplishments and the overtime you worked, didn't you feel yet again that you were never understood, never recognized? (*The client is visibly moved. The therapist then adds a third color to the ball of modeling clay with the two others.*)

You know, Gerald, I think that there have been many events in your life that have contributed to weighing down your life, because you were never given adequate help in dealing with them. (*The therapist adds new colors to the mass of clay already stuck together, forming a big multicolored ball.*)

Your dissatisfaction with your wife's behavior probably represents just a little piece of the whole. (*One more time, the therapist adds a piece of clay to the big ball, all the while paying attention to the client's reactions.*)

We can work exclusively on the marital problems you told me about. (*The therapist removes the last little piece of clay that he had just added to the ball and holds the rest in his hand.*) But I should tell you that I don't think that that would bring you the relief you're hoping for. What do you think?

Gerald:
(*Awkwardly hiding his tears.*) That's all in the past. There's nothing that can be done about it!

Therapist:
I don't agree. We can help the little boy—the 7 year old or the 10 year old—to better understand what happened to him, because he didn't really have parents to explain it to him.

Gerald:
(*Sobs.*)

Therapist:
That little boy believed that it was better to keep quiet and move on. He was really brave, but I think he would have suffered less if he had had the tools he needed to defend himself from such careless rejection. Do you want to continue using the methods of that little 7-year-old boy, or would you like to learn some more effective methods?

This type of multisensory thought process, expressed by the therapist using the modeling clay, leads to a much more rapid understanding of the facts of the problem by the client and promotes the establishment of a trusting relationship.

Example 2
Explanation of the Therapeutic Process

The therapist is working with an adolescent who says he is very troubled. He does not know what he wants to do with his life, he doesn't understand his mood changes, and he feels like a fake with the people around him. Part of the origin of the problem seems to be linked with the fact that he is easily influenced by those around him. He tries to conform to the expectations each person has of him.

Therapist:

(*Takes a ball of clay.*) Let's try to understand where your unease is coming from. Let's say that this yellow ball represents your color—your identity, your ideas, your opinions. (*The client nods his head and shows some interest in this "special" experience.*) Now, let's say that this green ball represents your mother—her ideas, her opinions. She has a great deal of influence on you, doesn't she? (*The therapist mixes the two colors.*) And your father's characteristics also are mixed with yours. (*The therapist adds a new color to the two previous ones.*) Then, there are your friends, who would like you to be a bit more like this or a bit more like that. (*He continues to add a bunch of different colors of clay representing the influences of his friends to the original color, so that the yellow disappears little by little.*) You know, when I look at this ball of clay, I'm not surprised that you feel so disoriented. We can hardly see you anymore. What do you think?

(*Given that, in general, adolescents are in a hurry to get results, the therapist can give the ball of clay to the client to encourage him to think about the time needed for the treatment.*)

Now, I'll let you take the rest of this session to sort out the colors in this ball and extract the original yellow part.

Client:

(*Clearly disconcerted.*) I'll never be able to do it!

Therapist:

Actually, I don't really think that it would be realistic to try. I just wanted to make you realize that I can help you find yourself in that multicolored ball, but it will take a bit more time than you were expecting to tell what is yours and what isn't. And it will take some time to learn to respect who you are, your needs, your ideas, and so on. Do you feel ready to get started?

The concrete aspect of this exercise allows the adolescent to understand the goal and the progress of the therapeutic process. In subsequent sessions, the therapist could also mention or show the ball of clay to help keep the client on track.

Example 3
Dealing with Bereavement

The following example deals with a father who has been living in a chronic state of mourning since the death of his 17-year-old son. The son had committed suicide by hanging himself in the basement of the family home, 6 months before the interview. The father had not yet returned to work because of his symptoms, which remained too strong. He still woke up every night hyperventilating, thinking that he had heard his son's voice. He had completely stopped paying attention to those around him, and by so doing was threatening the survival of his marriage. Everything about his manner showed his incommensurate listlessness.

Bernard:

I don't know what I'm doing here! (*Silence.*) My son is dead and, no matter what, nobody can give him back to me. (*Silence.*) It's too late. (*Completely defeated.*)

Therapist:

(*Softly and with empathy.*) Bernard, let me show you what it's possible for us to do together. You see this big ball of clay? (*The therapist places it in the client's hands.*) Let's say that it represents the weight that is pushing down on you since your son died. I'd like you to feel that it contains all the weight that you've been feeling since your son's suicide.

Now, part of this weight (*the therapist takes a small part of the clay from the big ball and puts it on the desk*) represents the guilt you feel when you tell yourself, "I should have known. I should have been there." We can help you with that part. There's another piece that corresponds to your anger toward your ex-wife, because she refused to let your son visit her that terrible weekend. (*Simultaneously, the therapist takes another piece of ball and places it on the desk. Each time the therapist takes away a portion of the ball, the client feels a measure of relief, of lightening.*)

Another part of the ball comes from…. (*The therapist continues, naming each component of the client's sorrow while reducing the size of the remaining ball of clay, until nothing is left but a very small portion of the original ball in the hollow of the client's hands.*)

And you're right. There is, in fact, a part of your feelings that no one can ever take away from you (*he closes the client's hand over the remaining small ball of clay, trapping it there*). That part represents the memories that you have of your son, the love that you have for him, the things you did together. No one can ever take that away from you. But, that won't stop you from working, or from sleeping, or from loving your wife. (*The client weeps bitterly, feeling deeply understood. The therapist lets him take his time to calm down.*) Would you like us to work on setting you free from the other parts, Bernard? (*Indicating the other balls on the desk.*)

This technique can also be used for interventions with any type of bereavement (job loss, breakup of a romantic relationship, etc.) Depending on the kind of problem that is involved, the therapist can also choose to ask the client to identify for himself the components of the ball, their color, and their size.

❈ Audio Cassette

The closer we conform to the psychological realities described previously, which form the basis for Impact Techniques, the more we will try to be concrete and use tangible and visible elements to reach clients using the sensory pathways normally involved in learning and changing. We also become more receptive to the tools that clients themselves offer to us. For example, what therapist has not heard a client refer to a "tape" or say, "I was sitting there with them, and right away the same old tape started one more time!"? But how many of you have thought of taking out that famous cassette to keep the client's attention focused on the subject and to help him to further explore his thoughts and feelings? Our clients' comments often indicate to us the images that they connect with and suggest the objects that we can exploit to enter their private universe. Our job is to be on the watch for these hints.

<h1 style="text-align:center">Example</h1>
<h2 style="text-align:center">The Powerful Cassette of Childhood</h2>

This technique using "the powerful cassette of childhood" will likely be applicable to the majority of your clients, because their problems very often stem from their childhood perceptions, at least in part. It is a simple technique but has shown its efficacy more than once.

In the following case, the client is very annoyed from the moment she arrives. Something appears to have upset her.

Louise:

(*Half-angry, half-disappointed.*) Well, I went to an AA meeting last night.

Therapist:

You don't seem to be very happy about it! What happened?

Louise:

There was a guy near the door. Normally, we shake hands or at least say "hi." But yesterday he didn't even look at me! And right there, the old tape started up again! I couldn't turn it off. The meeting was a complete waste of time.

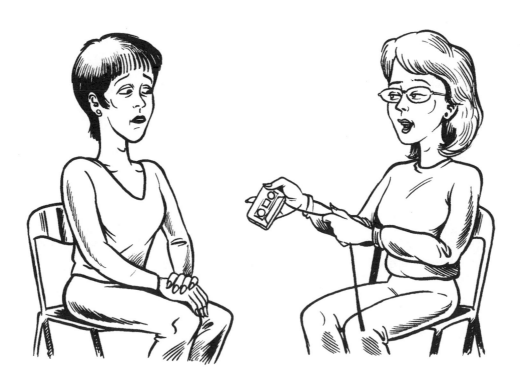

Therapist:
And what was the tape saying?

Louise:
Oh! It's always the same old tune:

"Nobody wants anything to do with you. You're good for nothing. You'll never make anything of yourself!"

Therapist:
(*Takes out a used cassette.*) Here, Louise. Here's your terrible tape. It's dated from 1961 (*Louise's birth year*) to 2005. (*The therapist writes the two dates on the cassette, along with the first name of the client.*) You've been listening to this old tape all your life. Now, how would you rate your satisfaction on a scale of 0 to 10?

Louise:
Oh! Two, at the very most!

Therapist:
Okay, so let's put 2 out of 10 on the tape. (*He writes 2/10 in the upper right-hand corner of the cassette.*) That means that eight-tenths of what is on this tape isn't true or useful to you. (*He writes 8/10 in the upper left-hand corner. It should be noted that this intervention, previously explained to the client, fits within the framework of Rational Emotive Behavior Theory.*) Now, Louise, what words would you use to describe this part of your life?

Louise:
(*Appearing to concentrate.*) Isolation…failure…fear…alcoholism.

Therapist:
(*The therapist writes these words on the cassette.*) Tell me something, Louise. Who recorded this tape?

Louise:
(*Still thinking deeply.*) I'd say that some of those words come from my parents and some come from the kids I went to school with. Probably some came from me.

Therapist:
From you when you were how old?

Louise:

Oh, probably very young. Six or seven!

Therapist:

Louise, I'd like you to give me a number to represent the psychological balance of your parents. Be careful though! I'm not asking you to tell me if they were kind or not, if they were hard-working or not, or if your mother was a good cook or not. I want to know how you evaluate them concerning their self-respect and their respect for others. Were they fulfilled and well-balanced people? Were they at ease with their own problems and with their own childhood? Do you understand what I'm asking?

Louise:

Oh jeesh! I'd say that both of them were about a 2.

Therapist:

Why do you say 2?

Louise:

Both of them were alcoholics. They destroyed each other and were very violent. Not with us, but between them it really got nasty! I was put in foster homes several times. Mom tried to commit suicide more than once. My father didn't talk; he drank.

Therapist:

We could call that a generous 2, then! Now, tell me: If your parents' mental health was about a 2, why do you give what they said to you the importance of a 10? Why do you keep this cassette, as if the messages they communicated to you were true? Do you think they are valid?

Louise:

(*Somewhat shaken by the question.*) I don't know. I never thought of that!

Therapist:

As far as the comments that the kids at school made or the judgments you were able to make when you were very small, do you believe that they are completely valid? That they were true, 10 out of 10?

Louise:

(*Once again dumbfounded by this line of reasoning.*)

Therapist:

Every time you listen to these messages and you take them for granted as true, it is a 6- or 7-year-old child or one of your parents who is running your life, and not you, a 44-year-old woman. You see, Louise, I think that it is about time that you did a major clean up of the information that is on your cassette. Here, for example. (*Pulling out a part of the ribbon of tape from the cassette.*) Here the message is:

"You'll never make anything of yourself!" That one comes from your father, right? (*The client indicates agreement.*) And what would he say to me if I asked him, "Sir, why do you think your daughter will never make anything of her life?"

Louise:

(*Still concentrating on the cassette linked to her personal history.*) He said that when he was drunk and angry because I refused to go the convenience store to get more beer for him.

Therapist:

So, I think it's time for you to get rid of that part of the tape. What do you say, Louise? (*When the client approves, the therapist cuts part of the tape out and throws it in the garbage. He also could place it on a chair that would then represent the father.*)

The therapist continued the session, using the prop to "find" the information stored on the tape, and to analyze and contest it. Some sections could be changed, while others needed to be completely deleted. It is also possible to assign some of this process as homework to the client, to be done during the week.

Many variations can be added. Among others, the therapist can ask the client to put the cassette up to his ear and listen to it, and then to say how he feels. This exercise usually reveals many significant kinesthetic signs. The therapist can do the same thing with a new cassette containing nothing but true information and use the physical reactions of the client as a reinforcing element to advance change.

▓ Video Cassette

For some clients, the source of their dissatisfaction does not come in the form of words and messages played in their heads, but rather in the form of maladaptive behaviors that seem to manifest completely automatically in certain situations. In these cases, it is more useful to work with a video cassette.

Example 1
Persistent Painful Memories

Ginette says she is unsatisfied sexually. However, it is more a case of sexual abstinence. She says she is incapable of sensuality, voluptuousness, sexual games, or even sexual pleasure. The words that best describe her experience are "stiffness" and "disgust." She freezes whenever a man approaches her, even with the best of intentions, and she feels disgusted with herself as soon as she even thinks of letting herself go. It became quite clear that the source of the client's problems was repeated experiences of incest during her childhood.

Ginette:

I often see images of my father when he wanted me to masturbate and kiss his penis. What disgusts me the most is that I'm sure that it sometimes excited me.

Therapist:

(*Takes out a video cassette on which she writes "Ginette, 1958–1968," to indicate the years when the incest took place.*) Look, Ginette, I'd like you to imagine that this cassette contains all the episodes related to the sexual contact you had with your father. (*The therapist lets a couple of minutes pass, to allow Ginette to mentally transfer her past to the cassette.*) Even if all of those things usually occurred in silence, could you give me a couple of key words to indicate what this cassette invokes for you—a subtitle that summarizes the cassette?

Ginette:

(*The client is in an almost trancelike state as she remembers her past. She trembles slightly.*) I'd say guilt…whore…slut…responsible…disgust…responsible.

Therapist:

I think that it's time to change the subtitles to improve the video and to make it more honest, more real. (*Very gently.*) I would put "victim," "fear," "sadness," "revulsion," "solitude," "lack of understanding," and "pleasure," but a pleasure that was forced by the need to adapt to a situation in which you were powerless.

Ginette:

(*Silent, but visibly moved.*)

Therapist:

According to you, which of the two groups of words corresponds better to reality?

Ginette:

(*Controlling her distress with difficulty.*) The only time I tried to talk to my mother about it, she told me it was my fault. She said, "You just have to make sure that you don't get in his way."

Therapist:

(*In an empathic tone*) Ginette, I think that your mother didn't really know what to do. But, if she had been capable of it, she would certainly have taken you in her arms and said to you (*addressing a small child's chair as if little Ginette were sitting there*), "Sweetie, I'm glad you told me. I'm sorry about what happened with your father and I will take care of it. It's something that Mommy needs to take care of with Daddy, between adults. I don't want you to ever, *ever* feel responsible for what happened between you and your father. It's not your fault. You had nothing to do with it and I will make sure it never happens again. Promise me to always tell me if anyone ever tries to hurt you. Promise? And never forget that I will always be here to listen."

Ginette:

(*In tears.*)

Therapist:

(*Allows enough time for Ginette to calm down.*) Do you believe that that is what your mother would have said, if she'd been able to?

Ginette:

(*Nods, smiling slightly through her tears. After a pause, she continues.*) I feel better now.

Therapist:

It's important that you get rid of the old version of the video. (*Ginette smiles while wiping her tears.*) You're honest enough with yourself to only want to believe the truth, aren't you, Ginette? Even if there isn't a lot on this cassette, the young Ginette established a lot of equations based on what is here. (*She writes the following equations on Ginette's cassette.*)

sexuality	=	bad
sexuality	=	guilt
sensuality	=	whore
penis	=	disgusting
man	=	aggressor

Are they something like that?

Ginette:

(*After a brief silence.*) Exactly like that!

Therapist:

I think it's time that we give this cassette back to the young Ginette. But before we do that, maybe it would be better to make a few corrections. (*She crosses out the equations on the cassette and puts it on the small child's chair that represents the client when she was young.*) Do you think that little Ginette will be able to replace those equations with what her mother should have told her?

Ginette:

I think so.

Therapist:

I think you will probably have to repeat them to her a few times. (*Alluding to the dissociation between the child and the adult.*)

Ginette:

(*Indicates her agreement while wiping her tears.*)

Therapist:

(*Gives a new video cassette to the client.*) This cassette starts this year. It will be the cassette of your sexual life for the next 20 years. What would you say to titles such as:

sexuality	=	healthy and natural need
sensuality	=	fulfillment, pleasure
penis	=	genital organ
man	=	living being

(If the therapist judges that it is appropriate, it can also be effective to allow the client to decide on the new titles to be written on the cassette.)

Ginette:

(*A bit incredulous in the face of this new appreciation of her sexual life.*) This all frightens me a bit…I don't know if I can do this. But, I feel older, stronger. I have the impression of having found a way to retake some control of my life.

Therapist:

More than likely, you'll need some support. You'll also need to accept that the first few scenes on your new cassette won't exactly represent the pinnacle of sexual fulfillment for you.

Ginette:

(*Smiles, as if relieved by this last comment.*)

_____

This case has been described very succinctly. There remains substantial work to be done. Nonetheless, this brief example has presented a number of options that can be integrated into a session using the video cassette technique.

Example 2
Back to Basics

Renée's dissatisfaction could be more accurately called disappointment: personal disappointment for not having dared to do what she wanted, namely, become a professional chorus singer. After finishing her university studies with brilliant success, she made some efforts to find employment, but gave up when no concrete offers materialized. She currently teaches music at an elementary school. Unfortunately, she gets little satisfaction from her work. She continues to pay dearly for having abandoned her dream, both in terms of self-esteem and general satisfaction with her life.

Therapist:

(*Places six video cassettes to the left of the client and ten to her right. He also places one in her hands. By the way, ask your friends to save their old, unusable video cassettes for you.*) Renée, the cassettes to your left are already recorded. They contain the 32 years of your life. They cannot be changed. Some parts are surely acceptable, while other parts are probably less so. How would you rate your satisfaction, on a scale of 0 to 10, with what you have recorded already?

Renée:

(*Making an effort to make an honest assessment by reviewing a host of images in her head.*) I'd say a 3.

Therapist:

Three…. (*Deliberately leaves a moment of silence so that the client immerses herself in her dissatisfaction.*) The tapes to your right are still blank. You can record what you want on them, beginning with the one you have in your hands. You are the one who decides. You can simply copy the ones to your left onto the ones to your right and you will find yourself with another 3 out of 10 in 15 years—or it may even go down to a 1 out of 10. It's your choice.

(*The client senses very strongly that her past is there to her left, and all that remains to be created is to her right. The experience gives her a new kinesthetic orientation, while placing her at the heart of the problem and inciting her to action. The therapist can amplify this reaction in the following way.*)

But, while I'm thinking of it, maybe there are only five cassettes left for you to record. (*He takes away the extra cassettes and puts them away in a cabinet, closing the door, thus sending the message that the client may have less time to accomplish her goals than she had anticipated.*) Or maybe, you never know—maybe you only have three left. (*He repeats the same action leaving just two cassettes to the client's right.*)

So, you can put anything you want on those cassettes, creating a level of satisfaction with your life that is a 2, a 5, or a 10 out of 10. And if you have only one left? (*Once again, he takes away the cassettes to the client's right, leaving her only the one she holds in her hands.*) What can you put on that cassette, Renée, to make it a 10? (*Silence.*) In your place, I wouldn't take any chances—maybe you only have half a tape left!

———————————

Example 3
Distinguishing the Child Self from the Adult Self

When something isn't going well, Julie habitually withdraws until the person she considers at fault comes to her with an apology. Her husband, the main victim of this behavior, complains that his wife's pouting sometimes goes on for 2 or 3 weeks. The following interview was conducted with Julie alone.

———————————

Therapist:
Julie, let's imagine that this video cassette contains the experience of your childhood. (*He places the video cassette on the little "child" chair.*) Tell me, when Julie was a little girl, what did she usually do when she was sad or angry?

Julie:
(*Searching through her childhood memories.*) She pouted.

Therapist:
Why did she pout?

Julie:
(*Surprised by the question.*) I don't know! I think that she was too emotional to react otherwise. She was afraid of breaking down sobbing in front of other people.

Therapist:

Tell me, Julie, was little Julie's strategy of withdrawing effective in dealing with her sadness or her anger?

Julie:

No! Just the opposite—I think that she made herself suffer even more.

Therapist:

(*Takes out a new cassette that he places on the "adult" chair.*) This cassette represents the adult experience; that is, mature ways of dealing with problems are on this cassette. When you play it, do you see how the adult settles a disagreement or an interpersonal problem? Let's take, for example, the incident that happened last week between you and your husband, when he forgot your anniversary. You pretty much used the first video to deal with that situation, didn't you? (*The therapist indicates the cassette on the "child" chair.*) What would you have done differently if you had used the strategies on the new one? (*Shows the "adult" cassette.*)

Julie:

(*Stares at the new video cassette for a long moment.*) I don't really know!

Therapist:

What do you think of: "Honey, I'm really disappointed and sad that you forgot our anniversary. It's always been so important and meaningful to me. I have the impression that the only logical explanation for your forgetting it is that you don't love me enough and that our marriage isn't important to you."

Julie:

No, that isn't it. I have the impression that he does it on purpose to hurt me because I told him at the beginning of the year (*6 months earlier*) that I wanted him to plan a celebration for our anniversary himself. And he accepted!

Therapist:

Okay. So, the adult might say instead: "Honey, I'm really sad and disappointed that you forgot about our anniversary. You had promised me to organize a celebration when we talked about it on New Year's Day. My interpretation of your behavior is that you did this on purpose, knowing that it would hurt me a lot. Am I right?" What do you think, Julie? Do you think that this reaction is more suitable? (*He can continue modeling the adult while asking Julie to play the role of the husband, until the conflict is settled satisfactorily.*)

Julie:

Yes, that's for sure. But I never thought of saying that. I said to myself, "If he loves me, he'll apologize!"

Therapist:

(*In a mature tone, without infantilizing Julie.*) That is what the little girl believed! (*Points to the first video cassette.*) Isn't it time to teach her that, even if other people love us, that doesn't mean that they can guess everything we are going through and everything we want? To understand each other better, we have to express ourselves clearly and not be afraid to repeat, repeat, and repeat. Do you agree? (*The client assents, very sincerely.*) What would you say to teaching that to little Julie? (*Handing her the second cassette.*)

Julie:

Yes! I'd like that!

———————

Example 4
The Active Child

Somewhat like the previous example, the therapist can also profitably use the video cassette to place the client in the position of a spectator or a co-therapist. This technique is particularly useful for children who are overly active in school.

———————

Therapist:

Jonathan, I'd like to play a game with you. Would you like to play with me?

Jonathan (six years old):

What is it?

Therapist:

Look. Here's a video cassette of Jonathan from last week. We're going to see what kind of week he had. Okay? How were things for Jonathan at school last week?

Jonathan:

He played with his friends.

Therapist:

He really likes to play, doesn't he? (*Jonathan nods his agreement.*) Were his friends nice to him?

Jonathan:

Not always. Sometimes some of them said that I was a pest.

Therapist:

Really? Why did they say that?

Jonathan:

Because I want to play with them but they want to do their work.

(*It is not important if the client vacillates between "I" and "he"; however, the therapist should try to maintain the dissociation in his choice of words.*)

Therapist:

Oh really? And how did the teacher act on that cassette?

Jonathan:

(*Still concentrating on the video cassette.*) She was always on my back and she kept sending me to the corner as punishment.

Therapist:

Really? Why did she do that?

Jonathan:

She always says that I bother the others.

Therapist:

Oh. And how did the mommy and daddy act on the cassette?

Jonathan:

They were nice.

Therapist:

Always?

Jonathan:

No! Sometimes they aren't happy when I do something to get punished at school and…and they argue with me, too.

Therapist:

Tell me, does Jonathan sometimes cry when he is by himself on this cassette?

Jonathan:

(*Somewhat timidly.*) Yeah.

Therapist:

Here, Jonathan. Here's a new cassette. It's still about Jonathan, the same Jonathan who really wants to play with his friends, but who tells himself, "No, I will wait until recess or after school! It will be hard, but I will try to force myself to wait." (*With a somewhat theatrical expression.*) Do you think that Jonathan will be treated as a pest by his friends?

Jonathan:

(*Really concentrating to try to imagine that new reality.*) No.

Therapist:

Will that Jonathan get in trouble with the teacher or will she be nice to him?

Jonathan:

(*Still thinking hard.*) I think she will be nice!

Therapist:

And do you think that Jonathan's mommy and daddy will be happy?

Jonathan:

(*With a convinced and convincing nod of the head.*) Oh yes!

Therapist:

Do you think that that Jonathan will cry when he is alone?

Jonathan:

(*Again tries to visualize it.*) No!

(*Overall, the therapist tries to describe, as accurately as possible, the child's reality, his needs and the means he uses to fulfill them. Then he tries to help the child recognize the cost of these strategies compared to that of more appropriate tactics.*)

Therapist:

(*Takes the two video cassettes in his hands.*) Which one do you want to take with you this week?

Jonathan:

This one! (*Rushes to point to the cassette of the "nice" Jonathan.*)

Therapist:

Great. Here's what we're going to do. I'll keep the other cassette. That way, it won't bother you. (*Sometimes, this sort of Ericksonian hypnotic induction gives good results. There's no harm in trying!*) You will take the new one with you. It will be a secret between us. Take the cassette and put it in your school bag. When you get to school, you can put it in or on your desk. It will help you to remember what you should do. Okay?

———————

The idea of having a secret can sometimes stimulate children to exhibit the desired behavior. The therapist can also reuse the cassette to review the week or to make needed changes during the next session.

Filter

The filter helps to show clients the importance of selecting the information that comes from certain people who are harmful to their well-being. Any kind of filter will do, but usually we use a coffee filter.

Example
Know How to Filter Information

Brigitte, a veterinarian, stopped working a month ago. The degrading attitude of her boss seems to be the cause of her depression. For unknown reasons, he was constantly harassing, humiliating, and insulting her since she first set foot in his clinic 5 months earlier. The filter is among the techniques that the therapist can use with her.

Therapist:

I know you've had a lot of scientific training. In psychology, we do experiments, too. Take this empty glass for example. Every time we are with people who are comfortable with themselves, mentally healthy and who say something about us (*here symbolized by clear water that the therapist pours into the glass*), we can take those comments and swallow them (*the therapist can sip the contents of the glass, for emphasis*). Generally, we come away stronger, satisfied, and nourished. Unfortunately, we sometimes find ourselves with people who are not very nice, who are frustrated, angry, jealous, and disturbed. Their words are usually pretty bitter and nasty. (*The therapist repeats the comments of Brigitte's old boss in an aggressive tone of voice and at the same time adds bits of trash and dirt to the glass of water. He then offers it to Brigitte.*) Here, Brigitte, have a drink!

Brigitte:

No! It's disgusting!

Therapist:

But isn't that just what you did before? You swallowed all the junk that your boss threw at you. And now you come to see me saying that you have digestive problems…well, I'm not surprised! You have to filter information. (*He places a filter over a new clean glass and pours into it the dirty contents of the first one. The bits of trash are trapped in the filter and clean liquid flows into the glass.*) We need to keep the things that come from healthy people and we need to intercept—and reject—the things that come from people who have problems. Almost always, those things have nothing to do with us and everything to do with the problems of the person who says them.

The discussion can go on to address the reactions elicited by the exercise and to help the client to distinguish well-intentioned people from those who are not. The therapist can also give the client a clean filter to underline its importance and to encourage her to use this technique during the following week.

In addition, the filter can be used to dispose of undesirable information coming from an ego state (we'll see more on ego states in Chapter 2). It has also proven to be a remarkably effective aid when working with children who are teased by their classmates or with individuals who have verbally abusive partners.

$20 Bill

The $20 bill is one of the most commonly used Impact Techniques. It can produce a truly major and virtually permanent impact for clients who, like everyone, regularly handle money.

Example 1
Self-Esteem in a Case of Incest

Many women who have experienced repeated incest feel that they have lost their value as a person. The repetition, to various extents, of this type of degrading situation in their adult lives appears to confirm their self-judgment. In addition, when they were still children, the mothers of some of these women blamed them for having provoked the situation, which clearly aggravates their sense of culpability.

Therapist:
You seem to think that you're not worth much. Let's try an exercise together. Tell me, what is this bill worth?

Helen:
Twenty dollars.

Therapist:
Exactly. Now watch carefully. (*He takes the $20 bill and rumples it as much as possible, throws it on the ground, and tramples on it several times while repeating the client's destructive soliloquy: "It's your fault. You went looking for it. It's what you wanted."*) Isn't that a little like what you have felt since childhood?

Helen:
(*With tears in her eyes.*) Yes. And I still feel that way.

Therapist:
And that is why you feel worthless.

Helen:

(*Quite moved, she nods.*)

Therapist:

(*Smoothes out the bill and shows it to the client.*) So, tell me, how much is this bill worth now?

Helen:

(*Appears surprised, but with a glimmer of hope.*)

Therapist:

It's still worth $20, isn't it?

Helen:

Yes, but it's very crumpled.

Therapist:

So what? If I go to the grocery store with this bill, how much is it worth? Five dollars? Fifteen? Twenty? (*Points to the small child's chair that symbolizes the abused little girl.*) During all this time, the little girl thought that she was responsible for what happened and that she was worthless because her father allowed himself to do all those things to her. Her mother said that it was her fault. Today, Helen, look at her. (*His attention is still on the small chair.*) Do you think that she really wanted to sleep with her father?

Helen:

(*Crying bitter tears.*) No!

Therapist:

(*Softly.*) Is she a hypocrite, like her mother says? Answer me honestly.

Helen:

Not at all!

Therapist:

Do you still think she is worthless?

Helen:

(*Shakes her head.*)

———————

A variant of the $20 bill is to take a sheet of paper on which the client has written her first name in large letters and a list of her positive characteristics. This can be done during the session or as homework during the preceding week. Once the list is made, the therapist proceeds in the same way, asking the client, while smoothing out the sheet, if some of the characteristics are missing or if everything is still intact. The client can then take the page with her and post it somewhere she will see it every day.

Example 2
To Stop Constant Self-Criticism

A colleague once suggested another use of the $20 bill. He uses it with clients who have the bad habit of always criticizing themselves and putting themselves down. The therapist associates the value of the client with that of the $20 bill and asks them to crumple it to illustrate their self-denigrating attitude. He also uses the same bills to evaluate the client's progress between sessions.

Short Fuse/Long Fuse

You do not have to find a real fuse to implement this technique—any kind of string, cord or rope will do. A short cord represents a short-tempered, impatient person, whereas a long one symbolizes a patient person who maintains self-control in all circumstances.

Example
Student in Difficulty

Many applications of the cord technique can enrich interventions in the school setting.

Sabrina:

I'm sick of school. I always flunk my math tests. I don't understand anything.

Therapist:

Sabrina, I think that the problem here is like having a short fuse. Look (*he holds a short cord in his hands*). This cord represents a person who has difficulty with math. She tries a little and then a little more, and then she quits. This one (*he holds up a much longer cord*) also represents a person who has problems with math but who is tenacious. She tries, tries again, keeps going, works harder, gets help, and finds all kinds of ways to reach her goals. (*The therapist can also write a list of possible solutions on a whiteboard.*) Which of the two do you think has the better chance of finishing high school? (*He holds the two cords up in front of the client.*)

Sabrina:

(*Points to the longer cord.*)

Therapist:

Which of the two do you think has the better chance of being at ease with herself?

Sabrina:

That one! (*Again indicating the long cord.*)

Therapist:

Which of the two do you think will be better equipped to face life? Because, you know, it's not just a question of passing math; it's also a question of being persistent or quitting when you run into other difficulties.

Sabrina:

Yeah, it makes sense!

Therapist:

Which cord do you want to take with you today? (*The therapist naturally gives the long cord to the client. He could also give two or three extra samples so that the client can hang them up in various places as reminders. The cord technique can also be a useful resource for parents of adolescents.*)

Card Games

Some of my colleagues have gotten excellent results using this exercise with older clients. The elderly often have many good memories associated with cards, which adds to the effect they can have when used in therapeutic intervention. In any case, I find that cards are very popular in many settings and are a practical tool for many types of clients.

Example 1
An Elderly Person Who Has Given up on Life

Six months ago, Janine was placed in a retirement home. Her children, who are very busy with their work and families, have taken progressively less interest in how she is doing. Since she categorically refuses to mix with the other residents of the home, she finds herself more or less alone most of the time. Her solitude and lack of projects have resulted in her losing her zest for life.

Therapist:
Tell me, Janine, since you were admitted to the home, how would you evaluate your life on a scale of 0 to 10?

Janine:
(*Appearing bored.*) Oh, zero!

Therapist:
Do you play cards?

Janine:
No. I prefer to stay in my room. Anyway....

Therapist:
(*Interrupts.*) No, I mean have you played cards before?

Janine:
Oh! Yes, of course, but….

Therapist:
(*Interrupts again.*) I'd like to suggest a little game. Do you know how to play poker?

Janine:
No, I've never played.

Therapist:
(*Deals five cards to himself and the client.*) It's very simple, you'll see. You just try to get a good hand—ideally four or five cards in a series or at least a pair. Look at your hand, keep the cards that you like, discard the rest, and I'll give you new ones to replace them. (*While explaining, the therapist discards the cards he is holding and sorts through the deck to find the four aces and a king. He does* not *replace the client's cards or wait for her to discard according to the rules he has just explained.*) Okay, what do you have?

Janine:
Not much (*she shows a pair of fours*).

Therapist:
Oh! Too bad! You lose! No problem, we'll play another round. (*The therapist repeats the same thing: deals five cards to each, doesn't replace any cards for the client and pulls the four aces from the deck for himself. Inevitably, the client reacts.*)

Janine:
But this isn't fair! You pull out all the good cards for yourself and you don't give me any!

Therapist:
Hmmm! Wouldn't it be more fair to say that you didn't ask me? (*Silence.*) You know, since you arrived here, I've been trying my best to offer you good cards, but you always refuse. I suggested that I could introduce you to some people here or to help you get started in the various activities that are available. You've given me the same response every time: "Don't bother. I'd rather be alone!" (*Silence.*) Nonetheless, I know that you have good cards in your hand. You're still in good shape, you have all your mental faculties, and you're doubtless a very dynamic person since you've done so many things in your life. You have all these trump cards in your hand, but

you always play your two of clubs when you say that everything is useless, that you would rather remain isolated, and that nobody loves you. If you would just use the good cards you're already holding and go after the other cards that you need, I know that your life could be transformed.

This intervention had a clearly positive impact on the client. In the following week, she had already improved her attitude. Imagine how you could use this technique with your own clients.

Example 2
She Who Lets Others Decide for Her

Judith, 32, is emotionally dependent and incapable of making decisions.

Therapist:
Judith, do you know how to play 31?

Judith:
No, I'm not much of a card player.

Therapist:

We can still give it a try, if you like. You'll see, it's interesting.

Judith:

(*As is her habit, she accepts the suggestion without batting an eyelash.*)

Therapist:

(*Deals three cards to each player. The game consists of reaching 31 with cards of the same suit, for example, a jack, queen, and ace of clubs. Normally, each player draws one card at a time, either from the deck or the card that the other player placed on the discard pile. In this case, the therapist deliberately insists on telling the client what to play.*) What do you have?

(*This game usually elicits the same reactions from clients as they would exhibit in daily life. Judith, for example, spontaneously shows her hand and plays exactly the cards that the therapist asks her to play, even if what he suggests is to her detriment. The therapist, meanwhile, hastens to make use of the cards that the client consents to discard until he has a hand of 31 and the client has almost nothing.*)

Therapist:

(*Knocks on the table with his knuckle to signal that Judith has just one turn left, which doesn't help her situation.*) What do you have?

Judith:

(*Once again, she shows her hand.*) I don't think that I have much!

Therapist:

Well, I've got a full hand! How did you like having your hand played by someone else?

Judith:

(*Judith reacts to the question as if she's been slapped in the face. Far from being angry, she has suddenly realized the parallel between the game and her life.*) I understand the message you're trying to send. (*Silence.*) This is really what I've been doing all my life: waiting for others to tell me what to do!

Therapist:

How do you intend to change your attitude now?

Judith:

One thing's for sure, I've never seen my situation so clearly.

Therapist:

What do you say, we play another game. And, this time, you make your own decisions?

Judith:

Yeah, okay!

The therapist tries to test the client by asking to see her hand and to tell her how to play now and then. If she really understood the message, she should resist, or at least notice that she is still in a passive mode. It may also be useful to repeat the exercise until the client is reliably playing her own game and is more self-affirming. The therapist could also end the session by giving the client three cards that total 31, which she can keep in her wallet as a reminder of her new self-knowledge.

Example 3
Magic Thinking

Mark is an alcoholic and multiple drug addict. The longest period of time during which he has been employed and had housing and a girlfriend is 6 months. At 33, he still has not finished high school. Despite everything, he is convinced that he's going to be offered a very, very well-paid job in the near future. This is what is called magic thinking.

Therapist:

(*Plays poker as in the first example, but this time gives the client replacement cards while keeping the four aces for himself. After a few hands, Mark reacts.*)

Mark:

Hold on—I don't understand! I can never win if you always cheat by taking the aces!

Therapist:

But I'm not cheating! I'm just taking the cards I need to have a winning hand! Do you have any idea what I'm trying to show you?

Mark:

(*Reflects for a moment.*) I think so. You want to show me that, if I wait for things to come to me easily, I might be waiting a long time. I have to go looking for what I need. Is that it?

Therapist:
Exactly! You see, when you go to an interview for a job as a paramedic (*the client dreams of being a paramedic some day*), you show your hand. But, there must be something wrong somewhere because you never get the job. I think that your high-school dropout card isn't helping you, and alcoholism and instability cards aren't strengthening your hand either. But, if you can manage to get rid of your bad cards (*which the therapist does while he speaks*) and you take the necessary steps to go get the cards you need (*searches through the cards in the deck*), you could find yourself with a winning hand.

Mark:
I have the feeling that I've had some of these cards all my life!

Therapist:
That may be, but that doesn't mean that you can't get rid of them! Everyone is dealt a starting hand. For example, you're 5' 9" tall and have brown eyes. Those are cards you can't change. But, if the instability, alcoholism, and high-school dropout cards aren't helping you, I suggest that you exchange them for winning cards. What do you think?

Mark:
It makes sense! Where do I start?

Therapist:
I think it would be useful to take a good look at the cards you're holding; and then choose the cards you want to keep, the ones you want to discard, and the ones you want to look for; and then decide how to go about getting those good cards you need and want.

———————————

Example 4
Blind Love

It is hard to find parents who are completely impartial with regard to their child. Theirs is always the best looking and the nicest. The same is true for people who fall in love. The object of their affection has only good qualities, never any faults. Unfortunately, this type of short-sightedness in love sometimes leads to problems. Here is an example.

Yolanda has been living with Julio for 6 years. He spends most of his time drinking. When he finally finds a job, he finds a way to lose it, either by stealing from his boss or by finding a way to hurt himself and receive disability insurance. His friends are his highest priority. That leaves him very little time and money to share with his girlfriend. Yolanda sees him from the inner perspective of "parent": she is convinced that he will change and become someone stable who will pay attention to her. In fact, she is waiting for a veritable metamorphosis in Julio, because he has absolutely no motivation to change.

Therapist:

(*Chooses 15 cards at random and places them face down on the table to represent Yolanda's refusal to see reality.*) Let's say that these cards represent Julio's hand—that is, his good qualities and talents, as well as his faults. You say that Julio has a certain card, say the king of hearts, that represents his desire to change and become more responsible and close to you. Is that right?

Yolanda:

Yes, I know he'll do it. He's really a talented guy who's full of potential. He may seem like a tough guy, but he's really a tender and sensitive man.

Therapist:

Okay. So, I'd like you to find the king of hearts in these cards.

Yolanda:

(*The first card she draws in not the card she is looking for. So she draws five or six more without finding the right one. The one she is so eagerly seeking has strategically not been included in the pile of 15 cards.*) The seven of clubs!

Therapist:

Isn't that a little like Julio? Every time he shows a bad card and contradicts your predictions of him, you tell yourself, "The next time, I'm sure that he'll make it!" right? (*The client is a bit hesitant.*) Try again if you want.

Yolanda:

(*Turns over another card and finds another low one. She realizes what the therapist is trying to demonstrate. She also feels a sort of sadness at the realization that she may never find the king of hearts.*) The five of hearts!

Therapist:

What do you think?

Yolanda:

It's just that you don't know him! Everyone thinks that he's a failure, but he's got such a big heart and lots of will power.

Therapist:

Okay. Then find the king of hearts!

Yolanda:

(*A little exasperated, not wanting to admit the reality of her relationship with her boyfriend.*) This is just a game! It doesn't mean anything!

Therapist:

And in real life, Yolanda? In your relationship with Julio, have you seen the king of hearts? Even once?

Yolanda:

(*Remains silent.*)

Therapist:

How many times have you seen Julio's bad cards? (*Yolanda still says nothing.*) I'm not sure that the good card exists, Yolanda, and if it doesn't, how many more years do you want to keep looking for it? One? Five? Ten? (*Pauses for few moments.*) I think I'll give you this card to take with you (*handing her the king of hearts*). I have the feeling that it may be your only chance to hold the king of hearts in your hands!

———————

Although Yolanda remained silent, the impact created by this exercise was nonetheless very real. It will be difficult for Yolanda to blindly hold onto her hopes without associating them with this encounter.

This technique is also useful when working with parents who have unrealistic expectations of their children, who want the perfect child—a completely disciplined and obedient adolescent who keeps his room perfectly clean. Those cards are simply not likely to be among those that a child or an adolescent is holding. In real life, when a parent is hoping to find an ace and finds just an eight or a five, it can provoke reactions as extreme as paroxysms of anger, which will only cause further problems. Using this card game in therapy can help parents bring their hopes to a realistic level.

Example 5
Setting Good Goals

Many clients come to us and try to convince us that there is nothing left to do for them, that they are fated to unhappiness and failure. Such was the case of a man who, after a serious accident, lost the use of both legs, his job, and his wife. Although these were major changes and very traumatic events, this man can still attain a state of well-being. It was as if, at the beginning, he had received a hand of clubs and had played it all the way up to the ace. At the time of the accident, he had reached all his goals, thanks to his own efforts and relentless hard work. Then a change in circumstances—that is, a physical handicap—had taken away those cards and given him new ones, this time diamonds. But he can still use all the cards, including the ace. Diamonds are very different from clubs, but not necessarily less good. It is a question of putting oneself on the right path with appropriate objectives. The goal of the therapeutic process can be represented by the ace of diamonds. This analogy lets the therapist make the discussion more concrete and can serve as a reference point during and between appointments.

Example 6
The Harmony Game

Although the harmony game can be useful in all types of therapy, it is most often used in marriage and family therapy. The hearts are the "love" cards—compliments, kindnesses, unexpected gifts, etc. The spades represent disagreeable and mean behaviors—anger, ingratitude, harsh words—that is, all the bad cards in a relationship. The clubs correspond to nonverbal communication; and the diamonds are associated with verbal ability. In other words, to assure a healthy relationship with others, each person should play some clubs, some diamonds, and, ideally, a few hearts when the occasion presents itself. And—as much as possible—everyone should avoid playing spades. The exercise consists of simply giving the same number of cards of each suit to each of the clients or, when appropriate, asking them how many cards of each suit they hold in reality. Then, the therapist invites them to "play" their daily life. The experience can make everyday acts more tangible and especially help the clients realize the active roles they play in their relationships with those around them. The therapist can choose to explore simple, uncomplicated problems or to examine more intensely conflictual situations, such as those described below.

Therapist:

(*After explaining the meaning of each suit, the therapist speaks to the four family members.*) You all seem to agree that meals are one of the biggest problems for your family. I'd like you to demonstrate for me, using the cards you are holding, how each of you uses your hand during mealtimes.

Mother:

(*The mother starts by playing a seven of clubs. The therapist asks what the card corresponds to.*) Maybe the preparation of the meal.

Lucy:

(*The youngest daughter continues by playing a nine of clubs.*) Usually, I help Mom by setting the table.

Father:

(*Puts down a three of clubs.*) Usually, I watch television while the girls are in the kitchen.

LuAnn:

(*Fourteen years old. She plays a five of spades. After a moment she explains, since everyone seems to be waiting for an explanation.*) I get angry when I see that, like he just said, Dad is always in front of the television instead of helping us. We all eat and we all work, so everyone should lend a hand. I don't see why only the women should take care of the food!

Therapist:

(*Interrupting the mother and father who were ready to speak.*) What exactly does the five of spades represent? How do you act?

LuAnn:

(*Makes a bit of a face.*) I get sullen, because there's no use talking about it! I've already tried and nothing has changed.

Therapist:

And you, Lucy? What do you do when you see the five of spades? What card do you play?

Lucy:

(*Thinks a little.*) Sometimes I say nothing and sometimes I try to play a low heart.

Therapist:

Okay, go ahead, play a heart (*which she does*). And you two? (*She addresses the parents.*)

Mother:

I'm often tempted to raise her with another spade…and sometimes I give in and do it. (*She is a little embarrassed to admit it, but is obliged to do so by the look her husband sends her. The therapist asks her to play a spade. Making the client actually display her negative behavior, even transposed in the context of a card game, helps her to become more conscious of her responsibility for her behavior in the family dynamic.*)

Father:

When someone asks me for a spade, I play a spade! (*Stretching for touch of humor, but none-theless recognizing that nobody is forcing him to play a spade. He places a spade on top of the other cards.*)

The therapist can use this exercise in many ways. In the first round, it can be used to clarify the costs and benefits of each type of card. The therapist can then guide the clients in a second round, going over the same events again, and asking each player to use a different choice of cards. In so doing, some clients may recognize their relative lack of hearts or diamonds, for example, and be motivated to try to acquire some. In short, the cards keep the clients' attention on the subject at hand while making them active participants in the therapeutic process. Note that the exercise is equally pertinent in all interventions addressing interpersonal relationships.

✕ Styrofoam Cups

Styrofoam cups have many possible uses, including that of representing self-esteem. The use of a concrete representation of such an abstract concept has many advantages. In each of the examples described below, it may be useful to give the client the cup after the session so that he can take it home or to work with him. Seeing the cup often during the following days can serve as a reminder and a reinforcement of the insights gained in the course of the therapy session.

Example 1
People Who Give Too Much

On that particular day, Nicole arrived in tears. Her sister—to whom she had recently given her living room furniture, her two prettiest dresses, and a new book that she hadn't even read yet herself—did not call her to wish her happy birthday. This was just one more incident in a long history of similar behavior. Nicole is one of those people who depends on the positive comments of others in order to feel worth something. These individuals give and keep giving to their own detriment and only succeed in undermining their self-esteem.

Therapist:
Nicole, let's try to concretely understand what is happening to you, okay? (*The therapist takes out a Styrofoam cup.*) Suppose that this cup represents someone's self-esteem. For example, if this person has good self-esteem, the cup is more or less intact, like this one. That way, when I pour water into it (*which he does*) it stays. In other words, when this person receives compliments or acts of kindness and affection, he takes them in, and holds onto them, and is strengthened by them for a good long while. But, watch carefully what happens when I pour water into a cup that has holes in it (*the therapist pokes holes in various places in the cup, including a big one at the bottom, making the water drain out.*) You see, as long as water is flowing through the cup, even if it doesn't stay, the person feels like they are filled, or fulfilled. But, as soon as I stop pouring water in, the cup runs dry very quickly. Do you see where I'm heading with this?

Nicole:
I think so. I think that I'm like the second cup. I constantly need other people to tell me that I'm a good person, that I'm wonderful, in order to feel that I have value as a person. But, as soon as I'm by myself again, or when I don't get compliments or when nobody is showing me affection, I feel empty and worthless again.

Therapist:

Exactly. I think that there are two problems with that approach. The first is that no matter how much attention or how many compliments you receive, it will never be enough because the cup has holes in it. Nothing stays inside, right? (*The client assents.*) The second problem is that the cup erodes, a little like the ocean eroding the shoreline over time. I think that, the more the water runs through the cup, the bigger the holes get, and the more water it takes to have just a few drops in the cup at any given time.

Nicole:

(*Deep in thought.*) I always thought that being super-nice with people and giving them things would make them like me. At least that's what happens at the moment that I do something. But afterwards, every time that they show up, it's to ask me for something…and when I need them, they're not there for me. What should I do?

Therapist:

Would you say that now at least you know what *not* to do? That you shouldn't give people things to make them love you? Next, we'll need to work together to repair the holes that you have in your cup.

Nicole:

That really helps me understand better! Can I take the cup with me this week?

Example 2
Evolution in the Development of Self-Esteem

After a recent break-up, Margo, a 52-year-old businesswoman originally from Europe, was feeling worthless. She also tended to generalize and see her entire life as a failure. The therapist knew that this was not true, having helped her at another point in her life.

Therapist:

Margo, see this styrofoam cup? I'd like you to imagine that it represents your self-esteem 20 years ago, when you first arrived in this country. It wasn't completely intact like the cup in your hands, was it? I'd like you to show me how you saw yourself at that time, using the cup.

Margo:

That wasn't a very good time! There (*she shows the bottom part of the cup, which is all that is left after she crushes it*), I think it was something like that.

Therapist:

Now, I'd like you take this one (*the therapist offers a new cup*) and use it to represent your self-esteem 10 years ago, after your divorce and after you got started in business.

Margo:

Oh, it was already pretty different. I think it was more or less like this. (*The cup is in better condition than the previous one, although it still has several holes.*)

Therapist:

This cup (*the therapist hands Margo another cup*), could represent the image you had of yourself 2 months ago, before you broke up with John. Could you shape it so that it accurately represents your state at that time?

Margo:

Well, it was like this. (*Margo leaves the cup almost intact, with only a few small holes near the top of the cup.*)

Therapist:

Now, let's look at this together. You came here today saying that you were worthless and that your life was a waste. That's not what I see! (*The client is perplexed and reassured by the accuracy of the diagnosis.*) Tell me, Margo, what did you do to go from the first cup to the second one?

Margo:

(*Visibly in deep thought.*) I stopped listening to everyone else and gained confidence in my own ideas. I started to believe in my own potential and to invest in it.

Therapist:

And you did that all alone because nobody, neither in your profession nor in your family, helped you, is that right?

Margo:

That's true.

Therapist:

And what did you do to go from the second cup to the third?

Margo:

(*Again, thoughtfully*) I think that that was a question of discipline. I took care of myself, by eating healthily and exercising. I allowed myself to take breaks, sometimes alone, sometimes with friends. I established some strong friendships based on my ideas and my efforts.

Therapist:

Margo, tell me, what do you have to do to move from the third cup to one that is completely intact? (*The therapist takes out a new cup.*)

Margo:

(*Somewhat morosely.*) Well! I think I first have to give myself a good shake and stop running myself down because John left me to go back to his wife. This exercise has really helped me to get back in touch with my strengths and aware of my own worth.

Example 3
Unhealthy Interpersonal Dynamic

After having listened to the couple in her office accuse each other and put each other down for several minutes, the therapist suggests an exercise to bring the clients onto a more productive footing.

Therapist:

Allow me to interrupt. If I understand correctly, you are both disappointed, sad, and angry because the other person never sees the good things you do. They always find fault and only talk to you to put you down. Do I have that right? (*The two clients nod.*) If you agree, we'll do an exercise together that could help you see things from a different perspective, okay? (*The two accept the suggestion with more or less enthusiasm. The therapist gives a styrofoam cup to each of them.*) Each of these cups represents your deepest nature—your values, your ideas, your needs, your identity. Write your names on the cups so that you feel more strongly that they really represent who you are. (*The two clients do so.*) Normally, in a healthy relationship, each should nurture the other with constructive comments and compliments. For example, Luke, you could thank Martha for the little things she does for you (*while speaking, the therapist takes the man's cup and pretends to pour water from it into the woman's cup.*) And Martha, you could thank him for taking the kids out (*the therapist takes the woman's cup and pretends to pour into the man's cup*). Your relationship is evidently not working that way or you wouldn't have come to see me. How would you show me how things are in your relationship?

Martha:

(*Thinking out loud.*) I think both of us put our cups out for the other one to see and to pour something positive into it. Instead, what we get is the exact opposite of what we're hoping for. Luke is constantly saying, "You never see what I do, you're never satisfied with anything I do. Clearly, according to you only other people are right!"

Luke:

It's even worse than that. Not only does she not respond to my requests, but she makes holes in my cup. Martha constantly tells me that I'm selfish, a sex maniac, and a failure.

Martha:

You're no better when it comes to insults. You call me a rotten cook, terrible mother, and you constantly complain that I'm frigid in bed. Do you really think that after all those attacks, I would want to make love to you?

Therapist:

(*Interrupting the argument*) Very good. Luke, is it true that you say those kinds of things to Martha?

Luke:

What can I say? It's true.

Therapist:

Okay. I'd like you to repeat it all while making holes in Martha's cup. (*This exercise helps the client take responsibility for his role in the unhealthy dynamic in the relationship. It also provides a visible and audible representation of the impact of his hurtful words and reinforces efforts to interrupt his hurtful reactions. If the client doesn't show enough aggressiveness to really damage the other person's cup, I recommend that the therapist play the role of the client, giving a more realistic version of the situation by poking holes and otherwise damaging the cup while repeating the insults.*) Martha, I'd like you to do the same thing. (*The two clients end up with very damaged cups.*) Luke, do you thing that Martha can be a strong woman, able to nurture you with love and attention when she is in that state? And Martha, do you think that Luke can be a great husband and fantastic father under the circumstances? (*Both clients look dismayed.*) I think that, wanting to be appreciated and recognized by the other, you've used a bad strategy. We can continue working on that together.

The therapist can then continue the therapy making frequent reference to the cups, both to control arguments and to stay focused on the goal.

✖ Sticky Notes

Stock up! They're cheaper by the dozen!

Example 1
"It's Got to Stick!"

Sometimes the progress that is made during psychotherapy sessions fades when the client returns to their normal environment. The following example suggests a technique to help consolidate the new insights gained by a client who suffered from extreme shyness and a lack of affirmation, especially in the presence of his father.

_____

Therapist:

(*This exercise is done with both the therapist and the client standing.*) Nate, I'd like you to take this piece of posterboard, on which I've written, "My opinion is valid and I want to share it with others to show my true colors." Hold it up to your chest. Isn't that sort of what you feel when you are here with me?

Nate:

(*Holding the cardboard to his chest.*) Yeah, exactly.

Therapist:

That message has really become meaningful in your life during the last few weeks, hasn't it? (*Nate agrees.*) First, you started sharing more of your opinions with your friends at the university. (*He leads the client gently toward a few chairs that represent his friends while Nate holds the cardboard to his chest. To add more realism to the experience and to favor an Ericksonian trance, he could label the chairs with the given names of the people with whom he has dared to express himself.*) You've been more assertive with your co-workers and at home. In contrast, when you are with your father (*he guides Nate toward a new chair, representing the father, and takes the cardboard out of Nate's hands and drops it to the floor*), nothing seems to work anymore and you become more or less like you were before and have a very hard time holding your own. Is that about right?

Nate:

(Fairly surprised by the precision of the physical description of his psychological experience.) Yes! That's it exactly!

Therapist:

Very good. So, this week, we're going to try something that sticks. What do you say? (*On a sticky note, he writes the same message that is on the posterboard and asks the client to place a sticky note on his chest or to keep it with him, at least in his pocket. A variation is to ask the client to write on the sticky note whatever best describes his perception of confidence and strength. The therapist then begins the tour of the chairs again, until Nate arrives in front of the chair representing his father. This time, however, the paper note remains stuck to his chest instead of falling to the floor.*) Do you feel a difference between this experience and the previous one?

Nate:

Yeah, I feel a lot more confident this time!

Therapist:

Do you think it will be easier for you to talk with your father when you feel this way?

Nate:

Yes…yes, I think so (*at first hesitant, then more sure of himself*).

Therapist:

Good! I want you to keep this sticky note and, when you meet your dad on Thursday (*the parents are divorced and Nate sees his father every other week, on Thursdays*), I want you to stick it to your chest, under your shirt, or put it in your pocket, so that it reminds you of what we did today and the feeling of strength that you have right now. (*Those familiar with Neurolinguistic Programming can add another physical anchor to this last instruction.*)

Nate:

(*Accepts willingly.*)

Sometimes it only takes a little helping hand to support a client the very first time he tries a new experience in order to help him achieve his goal. Since the therapist cannot always be present during these attempts, sticky notes are a great alternative.

Example 2
Tangible Psychological Support

Sylvia was supposed to appear before a judge to obtain custody of her children. Because going to court was a first for her and the case was very important to her, she was extremely nervous. She was so obsessed with the whole thing that she wanted the therapist to testify in her place. Unable to agree to his client's demand, the therapist gave her a piece of paper on which he had written a warm message of support (such as, "You are not alone. I'm with you," or "Don't let yourself be intimidated. You are right," or "Believe in yourself"), for her to hold in her hand while she testified. This type of "tangible" support was a remarkable support, not only in this case, but in many others. It follows the same principle as the old practice, now less common, of giving and wearing religious medals or scapulars. It is still just as powerful!

✦ Briefcase or Book Bag

Everyone, old and young alike, has accumulated tools for dealing with life's difficulties. Some of them come from our parents, other family members and friends, our formal education, or simply from hard-won experience. A real briefcase or book bag can be a useful way to symbolize the tools accumulated along the way. I have a suitcase filled with all my Impact props that I keep in my office and carry with me wherever I go to teach or consult. Until you have a similar supply, any briefcase or book bag that contains a number of useful objects will do to represent the concept of the toolbox.

A briefcase or suitcase can also represent all the unresolved problems that clients continue to carry with them. The baggage of these latent problems is often the cause of dissatisfaction with life, which can potentially lead to depression.

Example 1
Geriatric Clients

Her family and the staff at the retirement home were very worried about Mrs. Danville, who refused all contact with the other members of the home. Her obstinate isolation was pushing her little by little into a deeper and deeper depression.

_____

Therapist:
Hello, Mrs. Danville! How was your week?

Mrs. Danville:
The usual! Another week by myself. (*She complains that her children don't visit her.*)

Therapist:
How would you rate that type of week on a scale of 0 to 10?

Mrs. Danville:
(*With a forced laugh.*) Ha! A big 2!

Therapist:

(*Takes out her briefcase.*) I was thinking about you this week, Mrs. Danville. I had my briefcase and I was imagining that inside it were all the tools that you had accumulated or created during your life. You're the mother of eight children, you worked in a school for 35 years, you took care of your invalid husband for 25 years, you lost one child…I thought to myself, "Mrs. Danville must really have a lot of tools in her bag!"

Mrs. Danville:

(*She is touched and proud of this recognition, which predisposes her to listen carefully to what the therapist has to say.*) Yes, I've got a few!

Therapist:

(*Takes a sheet of paper and writes on it:*

"*Mrs. Danville, 1925–2005, 2/10*" *and places it on the briefcase.*) Let's say that in here are all the tools that you've accumulated since you were born. How can it be that there's only a 2 out of 10 on the briefcase?

Mrs. Danville:

(*A little sad.*) Hmm…I've always given all I had to give to my children, to my family, to everyone. Now, you can see what I get for my trouble! Not even one of them has the heart to come see me, not even once a week!

Therapist:

So, you're telling me that your briefcase contains all the tools that you needed to be happy; to take care of your children, your husband, and your home; and to do your work. Is that it? (*As she speaks, she looks inside the briefcase and takes out random items to represent these "tools."*) Hmm…I'm afraid those tools are not too useful anymore. (*Pauses a moment.*) But, I see some other tools (*taking out another few objects*)—organizational skills, social skills, courage, determination. You still have all these tools in your bag and you're not using them. They're all in there, aren't they? (*The client proudly affirms that they are.*) Do you have the feeling that, if you took out these tools and put them to good use, you could have more than a 2 out of 10?

That's what's really important, when you come down to it…. (*Mrs. Danville seems to agree.*) On the other hand, I understand that it can be difficult to put down certain tools (*indicating the first items that she took out of the briefcase*), especially when they've served you well for more than 35 years! I think that it would do no harm to keep them around just in case… but maybe you could leave them at the bottom of the bag, instead of at the top. (*The therapist puts into action what she describes.*) What do you say?

Mrs. Danville:

You know, you're making me think.

Therapist:

Do you think maybe it's time to do an inventory and revise the contents of your toolbox, in order to update it from the 1925 version to the 2005 version?

Although, the interview did not produce radical changes at the time, the description of the client's tools—using concrete, visual objects—gave the octogenarian something to think about. And, in fact, in the days following the session, the residents and staff of the home started noticing small signs that showed that Mrs. Danville was beginning to open up.

Example 2
"I've Tried Everything!"

Many clients believe that they've tried everything to find happiness. Suicidal clients, in particular, are completely convinced of it. The success or failure of therapy with these clients often depends on how quickly we are able to help them find some of their lost hope. The briefcase can be used effectively to show these clients that they may in fact have tried all the tools that are presently in their toolbox (the therapist having carefully labeled the briefcase with the client's name and date of birth), but they have not yet tried all possible tools that exist as solutions (the therapist can even designate another briefcase or suitcase, much larger than the first, to indicate this second group of tools). These are two very different realities. Simply becoming aware of the existence of more options often allows clients to regain hope and to continue in therapy long enough to obtain new tools, better-adapted to their present needs than those they already possess. In addition, no matter the clientele, it is always useful to remind those who may tend to forget it of the difference between the set of tools they have at hand and those that they can still acquire. As the saying goes, it is what we learn *after* we think we know everything that counts.

❇ Rubber Band

Rubber bands constitute almost irreplaceable aids for demonstrating the level of stress in the client's life or the level of trust in a relationship.

Example 1
Couples' Therapy

Some of you have probably been on the receiving end of disagreeable comments like, "It seems as if, since we've been coming to see you, things are getting worse and worse!" It's at those moments that it's good to have a rubber band on hand.

_____

Therapist:
(*Speaking to the couple.*) I'd like each of you to take one end of this rubber band with a finger and to show me how much tension you were feeling when you left here last week. (*Generally, at the end of a session, the couple has had time to air their grievances so that they usually leave feeling somewhat relieved of tension. That was the case with this couple.*) Now, show me the tension between you today (*this time, the indicated tension is so high that the rubber band is at the breaking point*). Notice, I'm not holding the rubber band—it's in your hands, the two of you. What happened this week to increase the tension between you?

John:

You had asked us not to talk about financial matters this week. Of course, we had hardly gotten out the door of your office before she started hassling me about how I manage my budget!

Susan:

(*Aggressively*) First, it wasn't as we left here. It was at the end of the week. And second, if you managed things better and didn't aim so high, maybe we wouldn't be in such bad shape financially! (*You understand why I didn't want them to broach the subject at home?*)

Therapist:

So, Susan, you talked about financial matters with John toward the end of the week, is that right?

Susan:

When the bills arrive and stare you in the face, it's hard to ignore them!

Therapist:

The assignment I gave you was not to not see them; it was to not talk about them. (*Susan emits a sigh.*) So, you pull the rubber band! (*The rubber band having returned to the relaxed position, Susan pulls on her end. The therapist assures that only Susan adds tension to it.*) And you, John, what was your reaction?

John:

Me? I don't accept being treated like a child.

Therapist:

Should I understand from that that you added to the argument? (*John is forced to concede the point.*) So, stretch the rubber band!

John:

(*Pulls on the rubber band from his side. Both clients' fingers are almost blue due to the tension.*)

Therapist:

Now do you understand why things aren't going so well?

The therapist can then continue with a productive discussion about the impact of the behavior of each person and to guide an exchange about the role that each had played during the past week, during which they had both contributed to creating and maintaining such a high level of tension that they rated the week as a 1 out of 10. Usually it is recommended that the clients continue to hold the rubber band during the discussion to add to the realism of the exercise and to facilitate remembering the physical metaphor between appointments. This can also be assisted by giving each client a rubber band to keep with them.

Example 2
An Evaluation

Melanie came to therapy to work on her anxiety. She believed that it was linked to painful memories of childhood that, oddly, she could not remember. After a more extensive evaluation, the therapist interpreted the client's anxious feelings as a consequence of elevated alcohol consumption, an inability to control her budget, and repeated angry outbursts at work.

———————

Therapist:
Melanie, take this rubber band and show me how much anxiety you are feeling this morning. The more stretched it is, the more it represents a high discomfort level.

Melanie:
(*Very anxious.*) It's terrible this morning. At least this much (*stretches the rubber band almost to its limit*).

Therapist:
Tell me, Melanie, were you drinking last night?

Melanie:
You know, I went out with Isabelle. Naturally, when we go out together, we always drink a little!

Therapist:
So, pull on the rubber band.

Melanie:
But.... (*she means, "But if I pull it more it will break!"*)

Therapist:

But, Melanie, you know that just metabolizing alcohol will increase your anxiety. Pull on the rubber band because you told me that you had a few drinks. (*The client pulls a bit more on the rubber band, not without feeling great tension in her body because of her fear that the band will break.*) The end of the month is coming. How is your budget?

Melanie:

Since I went out with Isabelle yesterday, I naturally spent some money. But I'll pay my rent with my next paycheck!

Therapist:

So, pull on the rubber band!

Melanie:

(*Really stunned this time.*) But….

Therapist:

But, Melanie, you know that each time you don't pay your rent the owner keeps hassling you, which really increases your anxiety, right? So, pull on the rubber band! (*The therapist uses the same reasoning regarding the outbursts of anger at work. The client stretches the rubber band to its limit. She realizes the active role she plays in increasing her own anxiety.*) Mclanie, use the rubber band to show me your level of anxiety when you are able to definitively control your alcohol consumption.

Melanie:

(*She considerably reduces the tension and feels a great relief at the same time.*) It would be like that!

Therapist:

Now, show me where it would be if you definitively controlled your budget so that you could pay your rent on time every month and put a little aside to take a vacation (*her income was high enough to make that type of plan*).

Melanie:

(*She again reduces the tension on the rubber band and again experiences a sense of well-being. The same thing happens when the therapist addresses her anger management.*)

Therapist:
Melanie, what would you say if we addressed these three problems first and that we talk about your past after that?

_____

By giving the client a rubber band and leading her to associate her tension with her concrete behaviors, the therapist is able to help her become more fully engaged in the therapeutic process. This technique is also very useful in cases in which it is not behaviors that cause the problem, but rather cognitions, such as in the case of phobias. For example, a client who fears flying does well until he finds out that he has to take a trip by plane. He then starts to tell himself all kinds of terrifying stories and thus increases the tension on his rubber band. The same thing applies to students who, in an attempt to flee their anxiety, go out with friends instead of studying for an exam or an oral presentation. These clients can thus visualize the process that brought them to a crisis and use therapy to experiment with the control of their emotions or behaviors as well as the impact that such control has on their internal tension.

The rubber band can also serve as an illustration of the future consequences of continuing to use ineffective strategies, such as fleeing situations that provoke phobic reactions or drinking to forget problems, instead of dealing with their difficulties more productively. The therapist follows the same pattern as above, but asks the client to imagine himself 1, 5 or 10 years in the future, still using the same harmful strategies, and to show the effect that would have using the rubber band.

Example 3
Trust in the Therapeutic Relationship

For years, Louise was the victim of incest from her father. Even though she is now 45, she has never spoken with anyone about this painful experience. To calm her fears and to help develop the therapeutic relationship, the therapist very effectively used a rubber band.

_____

Therapist:
I know that you're very afraid of talking about your experience. I'd like to illustrate the therapeutic process for you. I think this might help you. I'd like you to hold one end of this rubber band with your finger and I will hold the other end. You see, both of us have control of the rubber band. I know that right now the tension is very high because you are afraid. (*He pulls on the rubber band to represent the emotional state of the client, who thus realizes that the therapist knows how she feels.*) But, in a moment, I will let go of the rubber band and you'll see that it

won't hurt. (*The clients is more and more afraid, not knowing what to expect. The therapist brings his end of the rubber band slowly toward that of the client so that the tension decrease ever so gently. Then he lets go. The client is very relieved.*) That is how therapy will go. Any comments?

Louise:
That's very reassuring. (*She is now ready to trust her therapist more.*)

✴ Chess Pawns

Some of the techniques described above are used to address the same types of problems. The reason for this apparent redundancy is that each person, depending on his experience and his values, will connect more easily with certain techniques than with others. Thus, it is important to have all the techniques available so we can adapt them to the needs of our clients. These techniques using pawns from a chess set may resemble some of the techniques already presented. Therapists can use their professional judgment to select the methods best suited to the particular traits of each client.

Example 1
Sulking

Many people make recourse to the strategies they developed during childhood to solve conflicts in adult life. Take, for example, a young woman who, at 28, always sulked when facing even the most minor difficulties. When she evaluated the results of her approach to problems with her therapist, she realized that the days she spent moping earned a big 2 out of 10. On the other hand, she got an 8, and sometimes even a 10 out of 10 when she used more adult methods, such as more direct communication, as has been discussed previously. She recognized that this way of dealing with problems was more effective, but she still had difficulty throwing out her "comfortable old slippers." That is when the chess pawns were used to help advance the therapeutic process.

Therapist:

Annie, you say that, 8 of 10 times you sulk when a problem comes up. Is that right?

Annie:

Yes. It's too hard!

Therapist:

Very good. So, let's look at what kind of week you had. (*He takes out ten pawns—two white and eight black.*) The white pawns represent the occasions when you use communication to deal with conflicts. The black ones indicate pouting. (*He places the ten pawns in the client's hands, then takes one at random. He draws a black one and begins to verbalize the client's internal soliloquy.*) "Monday—what an awful day! Mark and I didn't talk all day. I'm feeling awfully sad. I have the feeling that he doesn't understand me and that he doesn't love me. I feel so alone!"

(*The therapist draws another pawn, again a black one.*) "Tuesday—another bad day! He must know that I am sad. If he loved me, he would come talk to me! I haven't done anything all day. I was too sad. I obsessed about the possibility that we might break up for most of the evening. I spent most of my time crying!"

(*Again, another black pawn.*) "Wednesday. I feel like this can't go on much longer between us. He doesn't understand me. He doesn't care about me at all. I feel so hurt; my eyes are red and he doesn't even ask me why. It must be because he doesn't care. When you love someone, you aren't so distant. Another wasted day, doing nothing, crying, thinking that it's all over. I slept badly. My digestion was upset!"

"Thursday. (*The therapist finally draws a white pawn.*) "Ah! We finally talked. I couldn't stand it anymore. I talked to him. I had been telling myself all kinds of nonsense! He was as unhappy as I was! Our discussion brought us close and I feel much better since I was able to tell him what I was going through. I slept like a baby, in his arms, with my heart filled with love."

"Friday…." (*The therapist continues, adapting his tone to the client's reality, depending on which color pawn he draws.*) Annie, what do you understand from this exercise?

Annie:

That's a pretty good description of what I go through. I can see that, when I dare to say what I am feeling, I feel much better, and when I pout, I completely waste the day!

Therapist:

Do you also realize that when you are ready to hold only white pawns in your hands you will generally have only good weeks?

Annie:

Yes, you're right! I should speak up more if I want to live 10 out of 10!

Example 2
To Err Is Human!

Often, at the end of a session, I give the client a few pawns, usually five. They represent the acceptable or normal number of errors for the week. For example, if I ask a father not to blow up at the members of his family, I give him five pawns to show him that mistakes are possible, even normal. No one is perfect. Clearly, the client avoids using all his pawns. Instead of feeling like a failure as soon as he has an outburst, he tries even harder to be more vigilant in order to save the pawns he has left.

Pawns can thus allow clients to avoid undoing the work already accomplished. In couples' therapy, for example, if one of the partners departs from the therapist's recommendations, the other sometimes uses this as proof that, just as they had predicted, there is no hope for restoring the relationship. In contrast, if both partners have already been warned that there may be setbacks and disappointments, but that this is no reason to declare defeat, therapy can continue with the hope of success. The number of pawns given can vary, depending on the state of the couple's relationship at the time. If they usually argue 15 times a day, or 105 times a week, 15 pawns would probably not be excessive.

The pawns also allow the drama of errors to be lessened. After all, it is not the end of the world and it costs only one pawn. For example, I remember an adolescent who was at the end of her rope and flew into such a rage that her mother ended up screaming back, "You always do this!" and "You never do that!" The young lady became oddly calm and said to her mother, "Okay! Fine! I just lost a pawn, but it's the first one in 2 weeks!" That thought immediately checked the stormy discussion.

The therapist can also refer to the pawns to evaluate how the preceding week went. It is not unusual to have clients happily bring back four out of five!

Contaminated Juice

Children who are easily influenced by others (that is, almost all kids) do not always understand the importance of their choice of friends. And since it is difficult to question their friends, it is often necessary to be inventive to get the message across. The example below is drawn from a scene in family life (not mine, of course! Oh, no!)

Jordane:

(*This is, of course, a fictional name!*) Mom, can I have a glass of juice, please?

Mom:

(*Mom is well prepared, because she had been waiting for an opportunity to help her only son understand the negative influence of certain of his friends.*) Of course, honey. Here you go! (*She offers him a glass of his favorite juice. Just as he is about to take the glass, the mother pulls it back and adds a few choice ingredients carefully prepared in advance—a bit of used cat litter, cigarette ashes, a used tissue, and some cat hairs. Then the "wise" mom again offers the juice to her beloved son.*)

Jordane:

(*Completely indignant.*) But Mom, why'd you do that? You always tell me to be careful with food and now you're wasting it!

Mom:

Yes, but I have a good reason. You see, the juice represents all your good energy. Sometimes, some of the people that you hang out with (or some of the thoughts you have) contaminate everything around them. That's why you have to be careful who you choose to be your friends (or what you say to yourself).

For even greater impact, walk away and let the child fully absorb the lesson. If you use this technique in your practice, you could explore further. For example, you could ask your client to make a list of the people he spends time with (by choice or otherwise) and use the juice metaphor to give the child a means of expressing the influence of each person on his life. Is Thomas like kitty litter, cigarette ashes, or good healthy juice that blends with yours? Do you know how to keep bad people from adding unappetizing things to your glass? (You can practice with the child, using role-playing and providing him with a model of healthy self-affirmation. Note that you will doubtless play the role of a bad friend, but perhaps you should also play your client's role to model behavior that he can develop.) Do you put bad things in other people's glasses or in your own glass? Do you know how to get rid of bad things in your glass? In short, this technique can be a pretext for an enriching discussion of positive and negative influences.

The same metaphor can also be used with adults, especially to represent the negative influences that may have been present during childhood or at the workplace which they should rid themselves of.

◆ The Soda Bottle

This technique has made more than one person laugh. Let's start at the beginning. I had a call one day from an acquaintance who I have a hard time saying "no" to. However, I was about to leave, I had a long journey ahead of me to teach a workshop, I was already late and here was Lucie, asking for my help. It is often at just such moments that my brain works most efficiently.

_____

Lucie:
I'm really having problems with my youngest. She's 7 years old and is very anxious.

Danie:
Could you give me an example of a situation where she shows anxiety?

Lucie:
Almost everything makes her anxious. If she doesn't get a perfect grade in a subject at school, it's enough to provoke 2 weeks of questioning: "How could I have not known the answer to that question?" If her sister sets the table and touches the lip of a glass with her fingers when she has a cold, my youngest is sure to panic: "That's it! I'm going to get sick. You did it on purpose. What am I going to do if I get sick?" To keep it short, everything makes her anxious.

Danie:
(*Knowing the child in question a little bit.*) Lucie, I think that some children are born anxious; that is, they have a tendency to slip into that kind of unhealthy questioning. You simply have to teach her to use her resources *for* herself and not *against* herself. Does she drink soda?

Lucie:
No. We never buy soda.

Danie:
She's surely had a mouthful of soda in her life!

Lucie:
Sure, when we go out for pizza.

Danie:
Does she like soda?

Lucie:
Of course, like all kids!

Danie:
Very good. Buy three bottles of soda. Shake the first one as much as you can and ask her to open the bottle, which she may refuse to do, knowing very well that the contents are likely to come spraying out and make a mess. But insist that she does it anyway. Maybe you will want to do this exercise outside.

Lucie:
(She is very surprised, but knowing about my "special" methods, as she calls them, she continues to listen attentively with an amused laugh.)

Danie:
Then, vigorously shake the second bottle and ask your daughter to open it, without letting the contents spray out. She will have to open the cap gently and reclose it slowly so that the pressure is gradually reduced. She could also choose to wait passively until the pressure goes down. For the third bottle, don't shake it up. Simply ask her to open it, which shouldn't create any problems. Then explain to her that she is a little like a bottle of soda. She shakes up her thoughts a bit too much sometimes. This can lead to explosions and messes. She needs to learn to stop "shaking the soda." In other words, she should learn to control her thoughts in such a way as to avoid building up pressure. If, for some reason, "the soda gets shaken" accidentally, she should be careful about how she "opens the cap." In fact, it would be better if she waited for the pressure to go down. Sometimes that will take just a few minutes, sometimes a few hours. One thing is for sure, the pressure will go down eventually and it will then be much safer to "open up."

This technique also works miracles with children who have a hard time controlling their anger. Do not hesitate to use the soda technique for any type of emotion that is excessive in your professional judgment.

Marble

Have you ever had the impression that a child was holding secrets inside that he did not want to share with anyone? It might be sexual abuse (often the first thing we think of when we speak of secrets), petty thefts that he has committed or witnessed, or violence on the part of one of his parents, his friends, or other significant people in his life. Here is a technique that has worked well in such situations.

Place a marble on a flat surface (your desk or the floor) and push it in various directions while asking the child to keep it from going beyond a certain area (for example, 2 square feet). Be sure to play long enough to send the marble in all directions, being sure that the child always blocks the way. Then explain to the child that he is doing exactly what he always does. He is keeping you from joining him, from moving toward him. You have tried all the ways you can to learn his secret, but he always stops you. Ask him if can accept the marble, instead of always stopping it and if he could let you hear his secret instead of blocking everyone who tries to help him.

☒ Bowl of Surprises

Another wonderful way of approaching the delicate question of secrets is to use a margarine tub (or other opaque container) and to put several objects in it, such as keys, coins, erasers, paperclips, etc. Don't shake the container. Instead, let the child believe that it is indeed a tub of margarine (or yogurt, or whatever the label indicates).

Example
Mysterious Margarine

Therapist:
What's in this tub?

Child:
Margarine, I guess!

Therapist:
You think so? (*The therapist then shakes the bowl so that the objects inside make some noise. The client is usually surprised, especially when the tub of margarine is taken directly from a refrigerator.*) Are you sure that it's margarine?

Child:
(*Still surprised by the noises from inside the bowl.*)

Therapist:
Do you know what is inside the tub? Could you try to guess? (*Be sure to have placed inside objects that the child will not succeed in guessing.*) That's a little like how I feel with you. What's on the label is very different from what is inside. You tell me that everything is fine—that's what it says on the label—but I feel that there is something the matter inside. Like you, I can't guess what the contents are; I can't know exactly what is bothering you. I can't help you if you don't open the cover and share with me what is bothering you inside. (*The therapist proceeds to do this with the margarine tub, to let the client feel the sense of relief associated as much with emptying the container—thereby putting an end to the noise inside—as with finally learning what was hidden inside.*)

_____

❈ Sponge

Invest in a large sponge like those used to clean bathtubs. Let the child feel its weight while it is dry. It will be very light, of course. Then, wet the sponge completely using a pitcher of water kept in your office for this purpose. Again, let the child weigh the sponge in his hands. It will be much heavier.

_____

Therapist:
Do you think that we can add even more to the sponge when it's heavy like that? You see, sometimes kids have a hard time at school because they are so heavy with sadness and secrets that they can't add anything more to their sponge, that is, to their brain. They can't learn. What do you think should be done to the sponge to let it take up something new?

Child:
Should we squeeze it to get the water out of it?

Therapist:
I think that is what you need to do, too—get out the secrets that you are keeping inside, so you can take up new information that is more helpful. What do you think?

Every child will react differently. The result is not always immediate, but you have given him an experience that will continue to affect him and to influence his thoughts. You can also reuse the same metaphor to continue the discussion in later sessions.

There are certainly other ways of using a sponge that you can devise. This simple object can certainly help you transmit many important messages to your clients.

Impact Techniques
with Chairs

CHAPTER 2

Using chairs as a tool in psychology is not new. Gestalt therapy is most likely the approach that has developed this technique the furthest. Impact Therapy and Impact Techniques take up this concept again and bring a unique touch to it. Whether you are already acquainted with this approach or not, this chapter should supply ideas for your next psychotherapy interventions.

◎ The Different Parts of the Self

Transactional Analysis (Berne, 1964; Goulding & Goulding, 1978; James & Jongerald, 1978) recognizes five parts of the ego: the Natural Child, the Adapted Child (submissive or rebellious), the Adult, the Nurturing Parent, and the Critical Parent. Some clients, although they do not use this precise terminology, also distinguish different parts of themselves. If we isolate each of these dimensions with the help of chairs, they become easier to recognize, analyze, and treat. For those unfamiliar with this approach, it is strongly recommended that they learn the basics before undertaking any intervention based on these concepts.

Example 1
The Square and the Semi-Freak

Jules never studied Transactional Analysis, but he could very clearly recognize his Adapted Child, which he called his "square" side, and his Adult (or his rational part, filled with humor and determination), which he nicknamed his "semi-freak" side. The first part, which had been dominant from the age of 6 to 16, a period during which his parents were almost completely absent, was causing him serious problems that resembled more and more an obsessive-compulsive disorder.

Therapist:

(*Takes out a small child's chair to symbolize the "square" and a regular size chair to represent the "semi-freak" to enhance the dissociation of the two parts of the ego. The client can look at his situation objectively and understand, describe, and modify it more effectively. This technique fits very well with the basic framework of Impact Therapy, which tries to equip the Adult so that it can act on the other disturbed or harmful parts of his ego.*) So, you say it's mostly the square who has phobias? (*Touching the small chair affectionately while the client watches, seated on a third chair, that of the observer.*)

Jules:

It's only him. The other part doesn't have any phobias—he's cool! (*Indicating the Adult chair.*)

Therapist:

And what does he tell you? What does he usually say? (*Again referring to the small chair.*)

Jules:

(*The more the therapist asks for details about each of the characters, the more deeply the client falls into a sort of trance from which he enters into each of the parts of his ego, without "becoming" that part.*) He needs to be perfect. It's a strong need for him.

Therapist:

Why does he think that he needs to be perfect?

Jules:

He thinks that people won't love him unless he is perfect.

Therapist:

What makes him think that?

Jules:

At school, the teachers and the principals treated him as the teacher's pet because he was perfect.

Therapist:

Did he like that?

Jules:

Oh, yes! He was proud of it.

Therapist:

How much satisfaction did he get from the recognition of his teachers and the principals, as far as love goes. Give me a grade on a scale of 0 to 10 to represent his feelings; a 0 would mean not at all and a 10 would mean the highest possible satisfaction.

Jules:

(*Appearing somewhat sad and hesitant.*) Yeah, well…I'd say 2 out of 10.

Therapist:

(*In a calm voice.*) What was missing for the little boy?

Jules:

(*Visibly touched, in contact with the pain of the Child, but at one remove from it because he is only an observer. Without this dissociation, the client would often be sucked in by the pain and it would be difficult to continue the process of understanding and modifying himself in a beneficial way. In Impact Therapy, it is considered important to make contact with the suffering of the Child within while remaining in the Adult state to be able to better participate in the healing process.*) A place to belong. My parents came to see me only twice in 10 years. Can you believe it?

Therapist:

(*To maintain the dissociation, he continues to talk about the subject, but using the third person singular.*) So, he missed his parents a lot. Is that right?

The therapist is not only collecting information here, but also trying to annul the Child's basic premise that he has to be perfect to be loved. He will also demonstrate to the Adult the naïveté of the Child's reasoning, in order to arrive at a more mature interpretation.

Note the rapidity with which the therapist was able to get to the heart of the matter. The client remains outside the evoked suffering, because he remains in the position of observing the small chair instead of sitting in it. This also reduces his resistance to talking about his experience. In addition, many clients feel a kind of hatred for their own inner Child. Their hostile sentiments decrease greatly when they look at the small chair with the eyes of an observer.

In some cases, the therapist may find it useful to ask clients to sit in the small chair, which will help them to immerse themselves in the feelings, memories, and emotions that are related to that part of their life. The therapist can touch the empty Child chair, talk to it directly, take it in his arms, and thus easily connect with that part of the client's ego, without causing a transfer. While the therapist is addressing the small chair, he is simply teaching the Adult how to become the healthy parent for the young Child, always alive and kicking inside each of us. He talks about the Child to the Adult. He shows him how to become a good Parent. Thus, the healing does not come about because of a transfer, but rather as a result of gaining insight and learning new skills through modeling and experience with the therapist. These techniques are closely related to the fundamental concepts of Impact Therapy; for more information about Impact Therapy, the reader may consult the books of Edward Jacobs (1992; 1994).

Example 2
Esther and the Pouter

Esther had a hard time controlling her sullen part (her Adapted Child). One day, her therapist was getting ready to leave on vacation for 2 weeks. He was already regretting leaving his client with the sulky Child on her hands, until it occurred to him to try the following.

Therapist:
(*At the end of the session.*) Esther, usually when you leave my office you leave with the sulky Child (*he places the small chair that symbolizes the sulky Child in his client's arms*). And she generally causes you a lot of problems all week long. (*He directs her toward the door, indicating that she should turn the doorknob, as if she was leaving with the pouting Child.*)

Esther:
Yes, that's true. (*Holding the small chair in her arms.*)

Therapist:
As you know, I'm leaving on vacation, so I suggest that we make a deal. I'll take her with me! (*As he speaks, he takes the small chair from the client and holds it in his arms.*) You haven't had

a vacation just for you for 38 years. I'd like to offer you one. The little pouter will come with me to the beach. Don't worry, I'll take good care of her. Okay?

Esther:
(*Hesitates, then enthusiastic.*) Okay!

This is much more than a game. The client, who has spent many sessions talking about the small chair, senses the Child who is in the chair and can describe her perfectly, both physically and psychologically. It is no longer simply a chair. When the therapist takes the chair out of the client's arms, it is as if he's taking the sulking part out of her.

It is not uncommon for this technique to give spectacular results. That was the case for Esther. During the 2 weeks that followed the session, whenever she started pouting, she realized right away that the little pouter was at the beach. Her behavior was thus positively modified.

Very often, the Adapted Child does not come back from its stay with the therapist or, at least not with the same intensity as before the experiment. One plausible explanation for this phenomenon is that the client often perceives the therapist as someone ideal. For a suffering Child, 2 intensive weeks in the company of such a wonderful person who can understand her and help her may be enough to cure her.

On the other hand, some clients may refuse to give the problematic ego state to the therapist. In most of these cases, however, it is only because they would feel sorry for the therapist. A client whose quality of life had been negatively affected, or even completely destroyed, by a disturbed part of himself will hesitate before placing it in the arms of someone who is not in the habit of living with those problems. It is thus important to reassure the client. You can assure him that you have at least 20 colleagues who are ready to help you in the eventuality that the little chair (or the Critical Parent's chair) gives you too much trouble.

◉ To Clarify a Decision

When a client consults a therapist for help making a decision, they have often weighed up the pros and cons already. However, most of them have not explored the kinesthetic information that is associated with their possible choices. With the help of chairs, the therapist can help them gain access to this gold mine of information.

Example 1
Psychology or Law?

Jasmine, 22, was planning to return to school but she was undecided about which program to pursue. Child psychology was as interesting to her as the law, but for different reasons. Separating the two options and associating them with separate chairs helped the client to clarify the two possibilities. In the example below, the therapist has also added the element of projection over time, to amplify the reactions of the client.

Therapist:

Jasmine, sit down in this chair and imagine that 10 years ago, you chose to become a lawyer. Now, you finished your studies a few years ago and you are practicing law. (*It is important that the therapist takes his time to give the instructions and describe the scenario, elaborating the details so that the client is immersed as much as possible in the suggested situation.*) I'd like you to describe for me, with as much detail as possible, the physical sensations you feel when you imagine yourself in that situation.

Jasmine:

(*Very attentive to her perceptions.*) I feel rather heavy. Yes, that's it: I feel like I have a weight on my shoulders. (*Silence.*) No, it's more like a mountain that I'll never reach the summit of. I can climb, but it always takes a big effort.

Therapist:

Is that a comfortable chair for you?

Jasmine:

No, it feels like something has a stranglehold on me. But, it's strange, my head feels somewhat light at the same time that the rest of my body feels heavy.

Therapist:

On a scale of 0 to 10, how would you describe how you feel in that chair?

Jasmine:

I'd say a 3 or a 4! It isn't very good!

Therapist:

Very good. Now, sit in the other chair and imagine that 10 years ago you chose to become a child psychologist. (*To accentuate the client's reactions, the therapist can put the "lawyer's chair" outside the office so that the client doesn't have it in view.*) You graduated some time ago and you are now practicing psychology. Again, immerse yourself in that experience and describe what you feel.

Jasmine:

(*After thinking for a minute.*) I have joy in my heart. I see suffering in my work, but, it's bizarre, I feel light. There's just a little something that bothers me in the pit of my stomach.

Therapist:

Do you have the same feeling of being caught in a stranglehold, which you described before?

Jasmine:

No, it's not the same. It's more like nervousness…no, sadness.

Therapist:

And how would you rate your overall feeling in that chair?

Jasmine:

Hmm…an 8! Yes, a solid 8!

The responses collected from the client after she has observed her multisensorial reactions add rich awareness to her decision-making process. The experience can also continue, to further develop the information supplied by the client until she has identified the meaning of the physical sensations she feels.

Example 2
My Boss or My Husband?

"Should I stay with my husband or leave him to move in with my boss?" A pretty serious question, isn't it? Which is doubtless why the client was having so much trouble making a decision. Chair work proved highly rewarding.

Therapist:

Kate, imagine that this chair represents your decision to stay with your husband Joel and that one represents your future life with Michael, your boss. Please have a seat in the first chair. (*The client sits on the chair that favors her husband. The therapist takes the other chair and removes it from the room to really give the client the feeling that a "yes" in favor of her husband also means the loss of someone dear to her from her daily life.*) Okay, you've made your choice; you've chosen to stay with your husband. Michael is no longer a part of your life. That's ancient history. (*The repetition is deliberate. It serves to make the client as conscious as possible of the situation described. If there are children involved, they should be incorporated into the scenario using empty chairs, placing them so that they represent the reality of the relationships as closely as possible.*) Describe what is happening inside you. How do you feel in this situation?

Kate:

(*Tunes in to her own feelings.*) It's calm, but unsatisfying. I know that I will eventually look for another Michael.

Therapist:

(*The therapist could continue to question the client about that possible reality, but, for purposes of this book, I will continue to explain the technique.*) What number would you give me to express how you feel in that chair?

Kate:

A 5, but sliding down toward a 0!

Therapist:

(*Brings back the chair that he had taken out, asks the client to sit in it, and takes the "husband chair" outside the office.*) Imagine that you've chosen to leave Joel for Michael. You are now living with Michael. How do you feel in that situation?

Kate:

(*She appears to make a mental shift to the new perspective.*) I feel alive! As if everything is sparkling. I'm also a little bit afraid, but I know that Michael and I communicate well. We'll be able to share our most difficult emotions. It's a very different life…much more dynamic. It makes me feel good.

Therapist:

How do you rate it, from 0 to 10?

Kate:
(*After a moment's hesitation.*) An 8! And this time, it's moving toward 10!
_____

The "neutral chair," described next, could be used to complete this technique. The client would be asked to objectively judge the value of the arguments made for the two options. Also note that substantial emotional and cognitive information may emerge with the kinesthetic sensations, adding new elements to the discussion.

◎ The Chair of Rationality or the Neutral Chair

Everyone knows that the person most closely involved in a situation is the worst judge of its objective reality. Which is why many people seek professional help—they want to put things in perspective and distinguish good from bad, all very objectively. The chair of rationality or the neutral chair is a very effective, even indispensable tool in these cases.

Example 1
Hatred of Men

A woman's hostility toward men completely poisons her life.

_____

Therapist:
How can I help you?

Stephanie:
It's very simple. My problem is men. I think that they are all disgusting and that they can be dangerous if we don't do what they want us to.

Therapist:

Oh, I see. Let's take a moment to do a little exercise. Would you please sit in this chair? Let's say that this is the neutral chair. You are no longer Stephanie, but someone outside her and rational, who doesn't know her at all. Okay?

Stephanie:

(*Sits in the neutral chair.*)

Therapist:

(*Writes the sentence just uttered by the client on a whiteboard.*) What do you think of this sentence?

Stephanie:

(*As soon as the client is dissociated from her emotions, she usually develops a more objective view of her own situation. Stephanie was in fact surprised to realize that the sentence suddenly didn't make sense.*) I have to admit that it seems a bit excessive.

Therapist:

(*With a touch of humor.*) Oh really?

Stephanie:

It's weird, from here, I don't see things the same way at all.

Therapist:

I'm guessing that the person that I spoke to a few minutes ago has had some bad experiences with men.

Stephanie: (*Quite surprised by the therapist's accurate interpretation.*)

Therapist:

Since you say that some of the statements in this sentence seem to be exaggerations, what would be a more reasonable belief, in your opinion?

———————

The therapist can continue to use the neutral chair throughout the process to help the client develop a more realistic perspective on her experiences and her opinions.

Example 2
Questioning Parental Labels

Although the impact of comments hurled by parents can often leave wounds, people can succeed in attenuating their effects. One great way to do so is to lead the client to question the hurtful words by experiencing the parent's reality at the moment that they made the comments. The neutral chair is once again an appropriate technique for this process.

Francine:

(*In tears, talking about her mother.*) She beat me and said that she didn't know what she had done to God that He saw fit to give her a daughter like me. She said I was a monster.

Therapist:

Francine, I'd like you to come sit in this chair for a moment (*indicating a chair next to the one where Francine was sitting.*) Let's say that this is a neutral chair. You are no longer Francine, but someone from outside the family, someone who can judge the situation without being involved. Do you understand? (*The client indicates that she is ready to adopt the new role.*) What do you think of this little girl? (*Shows a small child's chair to represent little Francine, at the time when she was brutalized by her mother.*)

Francine:

(*Does not answer, taking the time needed to enter into her new role.*)

Therapist:

(*Seeing the difficulty the client is having in inhabiting the new personality, poses some detailed questions to ease the transition from one role to the other.*) Do you think she is a monster?

Francine:

(*With conviction.*) No, she is not a monster.

Therapist:

Do you think that she deserves to be hit?

Francine:

(*With a lot of emotion.*) No, she is a good little girl.

Therapist:
What do you mean by that?

Francine:
She is sweet and doesn't want anything bad to happen to anyone. She is a sensitive child…intelligent…she is very kind.

Therapist:
Why do you think her mother hits her? (*Places a full-size chair to represent the mother.*)

Francine:
(*With knitted eyebrows.*) I think she is sick.

Therapist:
Sick?

Francine:
Yes…it's as if her brain goes off track sometimes.

Therapist:
Does she really think that Francine is a monster?

Francine:
No. I suppose that she needs some rest, to be alone. She's a woman who doesn't have a lot of energy or inner resources. The children are too much for her. And even if they spent all day just sitting, without talking or moving, I have the feeling that it would still be too much for her.

In this example, we can see that the neutral chair can calm the client while letting her gain access to very pertinent information. The objectivity that she is able to gain during this exercise also helps her to better develop the Adult portion of her ego, as described in Transactional Analysis.

◉ Empty Chairs

I have always envied the counseling professionals who visit their clients in their normal milieu. I think that that type of intervention saves a lot of time. On the one hand, one gets a better reading of the client's reality and, on the other hand, the client behaves much more naturally than they would in a therapist's office. It is fascinating to see the differences between the reactions of clients in their daily life and the reactions they exhibit when within the four walls of our offices.

Nonetheless, given that the majority of professionals are obliged to settle for appointments in their offices, empty chairs can become important elements to reconstitute the normal setting in which the client lives. No matter what type of therapy is being done (marital, individual, group, etc.), the therapist can associate a chair with each of the important people who are absent but identified during the interview. In so doing, the client feels the presence of the others, which increases the validity of his or her responses.

Let's look at the example of an interview in which the client talks about her anger and bitterness toward her ex-husband. As soon as the therapist placed a chair representing this man next to the client, she moved to the other side of the room. This type of nonverbal reaction confirms the significant effect of the empty chair.

Another client had linked the eight chairs in his therapist's office with various people who were close to him. At every session, he spontaneously reestablished this link, saying, for instance, "It's his fault," pointing to a particular chair. This reaction tested the therapist's memory, who had to remember who that chair represented. The client saw and sensed the person in question. The office had become inhabited by these imaginary—but also very real—people.

Sometimes the projection is more successful when the therapist adds an object to the empty chair. For example, a bottle of beer could be placed on a chair to represent the alcoholic father or a book placed on a bench could represent the intellectual mother. The name of a person written on a sheet of paper taped to the back of a chair can also evoke that person. Then there are some clients who find it easier to imagine a person sitting in the chair when it is completely empty.

Once the important people in the client's life are installed in the various chairs in the office, the therapist can ask him about their reactions or to inhabit each of the personalities by moving from one chair to another. The empty chairs thus become valuable tools that add dynamism, realism, and variety to the therapeutic sessions.

◎ Role-Playing

The examples in the preceding chapter have already given a glimpse of the kinds of role-playing used in Impact Therapy. The majority of them have been the result of staging in which the different parts of the self were involved. The following examples will further develop role-playing that involves other people.

Example
Settle a Conflict with an Absent Person

Louis's parents divorced when he was 10 years old. The break-up was hard on him, especially because his father never called him on the phone again. The father was always very polite on the phone when his son called, but he never took the initiative to call himself, not even on his son's birthday. Louis interpreted this behavior as a sign of rejection and indifference, and he had the impression that his father, who was a successful professional, was ashamed of him. In fact, at 19 Louis did not know what he wanted to become and, in addition, he had a lot of trouble at school.

Therapist:
Louis, I'd like to suggest an exercise. I think that it might help you to understand what is happening between you and your father better. It might not be easy, but I will help you. What do you say?

Louis:
What is it?

Therapist:
Let's say that this chair represents your father (*places a chair about 4 feet in front of Louis*). What would you like to say to him?

Louis:
I don't know. (*He feels a bit embarrassed by the abruptness of this turn of affairs.*)

Therapist:
Would you like to know whether he loves you? So, ask him, "Dad, do you love me?"

Louis:

(*At the therapist's insistence, somewhat mechanically repeats the same words.*) Dad, do you love me?

Therapist:

Now, sit in his place and answer Louis's question.

Louis:

(*Sitting in the father's chair, the response comes to him spontaneously.*) Of course, I love you! Why do you think that I've been paying for you for 19 years?

Therapist:

Okay. Now go back to your chair and talk to your father.

Louis:

(*Turning toward the therapist.*) That's not what I want!

Therapist:

What do you want?

Louis:

I want him to call me, to do things together, to show me that I'm worth something to him.

Therapist:

So, tell him!

Louis:

(*It is apparent that the experience is becoming less and less of a game and more and more real.*) That isn't what I want. I'd have liked it if, during all these years, you had called me, asked how things were going, taken me out on my birthday. If you had done something other than just pay!

Therapist:

(*Signals the client to change chairs and return to the father's place.*)

Louis:

(*Sits for a moment in the chair, listening for what his father might feel, and then addresses the therapist.*) He doesn't say anything!

Therapist:
Sit in your chair again. (*Louis does so.*) Would you like to ask him why he never called? Okay, go ahead. Ask him.

Louis:
Why didn't you ever call?

Therapist:
(*Indicates that the client should change chairs.*)

Louis:
(*In the father's chair.*) He doesn't answer.

Therapist:
Tell me, does he love Louis?

Louis:
(*Still in the father's chair.*) Yes, he loves him. But every time I sit in his chair I feel as if there is a solid stone wall around me.

Therapist:
Why doesn't he tell Louis that he loves him?

Louis:
He feels too vulnerable and incapable of saying that kind of thing. He is stuck in this trap with stone walls.

Therapist:
Is he ashamed of Louis? (*The therapist tries to defuse Louis's irrational thoughts by confronting him with his father's reality.*)

Louis:
(*Still trying to tune in to the sensations in the father's chair.*) No, that isn't it.

Therapist:
Would he call more often, take his son out on his birthday, and tell him that he loved him if his son performed better in school?

Louis:

No. No, that wouldn't change anything about the way he acts toward him.

Therapist:

Louis, sit here now. Let's say that this is a neutral chair. (*The therapist and the client are now seated side by side looking at the two chairs involved in the role-playing.*) You see, I have two opposing realities here. One says, "He doesn't love me. He is ashamed of me. He doesn't call me because he wants nothing to do with me." The other one says, "I love him. I'm not ashamed of him. I don't call because I'm a prisoner inside my stone walls." Louis, one of these chairs represents reality (*the therapist writes 2+2=4 on a self-adhesive note paper*) and the other represents imagination (*he takes out another note and writes 2+2=9*). I'd like to know where I should stick these labels. Which chair corresponds to 2+2=4?

Louis:

(*Realizes that it is the father's chair and signals the therapist to put the note there.*)

Therapist:

(*Sticks the two notes on the appropriate chairs.*) Louis, you can still believe that 2+2=9, but you know that it's false. The truth is that your father loves you and that he appreciates you a lot, but he is uncomfortable with himself. You can leave here and keep sitting on the chair where you tell yourself a bunch of lies or you can simply choose to sit on the chair of truth. Which one do you prefer?

The client left the interview not only having heard a bunch of words, but having had an experience that provided images that he will remember and integrate into his personal life experience.

◎ Time

A man does not believe in himself because, when he was 10, he flunked a year in school. A woman hates all men because, during her adolescence, her father sexually abused her. Another woman does not want to have another child because her first child died in a car accident. Do you see the similarity between these cases? All of these people stopped living after a bad experience. Instead of dealing with their problem, they have simply cut off all contact with anything that could wake up their horrible pain. That's a bad idea. Such people rapidly find themselves with two problems: the original problem and that created by the bad strategies used to face the first one.

Example
Couple at Odds after an Affair

The couple described here had been living in a veritable hell for 8 years. Tony had frequented prostitutes for 2 years during their marriage in order to finally explore his sexuality, which he had been obliged to put on hold during his adolescence owing to a heavy load of family responsibilities. After 2 years of intensive debauchery, he decided to confess all to his wife. He was sure that she would forgive him because she was well aware of the circumstances of his childhood. That was not the case. Instead, Nadine vehemently attacked him and, even after 8 years had gone by, Tony still could not come in the house without his wife insulting him, swearing, and screaming as if it was the day after his confession. It had become an intolerable situation for the entire household.

Therapist:
(*He doesn't even have time to pose an opening question such as "What seems to be the problem?" before Nadine starts venting a torrent of complaints.*)

Nadine:
I'll tell you what's the matter. You're looking at a disgusting man, the most revolting, the most sickening of his entire species. It takes a pig, a maniac like him to be capable of….

Therapist:
(*Nadine goes on speaking. Realizing that he would not be able to interrupt her despite being firm, he decided to get Tony, who was hunched over, clearly showing his penitence, out of the room. Nadine's whining litany was just punishing him. As soon as Tony had left the room, as the therapist had asked him to do, Nadine calmed down. The therapist was finally able to participate in the discussion.*) Nadine, what year did your husband admit all this to you?

Nadine:
The 2nd of July, 1997. At 10 in the morning.

Therapist:
(*Writes "1997" on a self-adhesive note and sticks it to the back of a chair.*) Nadine, what's today's date?

Nadine:
(*The simplicity of the question makes her look at him with an exasperated air.*) The 3rd of September, 2005!

Therapist:
(*Writes "2005" on another note and sticks it to the back of another chair facing her.*) Nadine, what chair are you sitting on?

_____

The client reacted strongly to this demonstration. She realized that for the last 8 years she hadn't progressed from the scene of that horrible morning of July 2, that she had deprived herself of living fully, evolving, learning, laughing, loving. Every time she saw her husband or thought of sharing something with him, she saw July 2 all over again. Pursuing projects together? It was unthinkable because of July 2. This woman, like so many others, had stopped living after a powerful event. By so doing, she had lost 8 nonrefundable years of her life.

To amplify the impact of the intervention, the therapist took out his calculator to convert the years into irreplaceable minutes: 8 years × 365 days × 24 hours × 60 minutes = 4,204,800 minutes! That's a lot. Way too much. After listening to the client's comments, the therapist suggested that he help her to change the chair she occupied, on two conditions: no more tirades in his office or at home. Having recognized what her attitude had cost her since 1997, she readily agreed to the offer and respected the conditions.

◉ Role Reversal and Co-Therapy

The following are two examples to illustrate the benefits associated with role-reversal techniques.

Example 1
A Secret Well-Hidden for 50 Years

When Jerry, 65, consulted a therapist, he said he was motivated by a desire for personal growth. After three or four sessions, the therapist had the feeling that Jerry was hiding something very important.

Therapist:

Jerry, I'd like to suggest a somewhat different exercise today. Come sit on this chair next to me. Today, you are going to be my co-therapist and together we will try to help Jerry. Okay?

Jerry:

(*Sits next to the therapist, and the two face the empty chair recently occupied by Jerry.*) We can try!

Therapist:

What do you think of Jerry?

Jerry:

(*In his new role as co-therapist.*) In my opinion, he has a problem with self-esteem.

Therapist:

Yes, that's also my opinion. What do you think it's due to?

Jerry:

I think it started in his childhood!

Therapist:

About when, in your view?

Jerry:

Probably during his adolescence!

Therapist:

Do you think he is telling us everything?

Jerry:

Not really.

Therapist:

Why do you think that is?

Jerry:

Maybe he thinks that it's something one doesn't talk about....

Therapist:

....something one doesn't talk about. (*Empathetic.*) What is it that one doesn't talk about? Something sexual maybe? What do you think?

Jerry:

(*A little hesitant, his voice suddenly husky.*) That could be!

Therapist:

Do you have the feeling that he was always convinced that he had to be quiet about it and that, consequently, he has been a prisoner of his secret all his life?

Jerry:

(*Thinking.*) That's what it looks like.

Therapist:

Do you think it would be beneficial for him to share his secret with someone he trusted, like me, for example, who could help him to better understand and interpret what happened?

Jerry:

(*Appears to imagine the possibility for the first time.*) It's an interesting idea.

Therapist:

How could we help him to talk about the things that seem so hard for him?

_____

In short, the therapist can pose all the questions he wishes. The client, who has become the co-therapist, can't help but respond and supply the means to achieve the desired result. In addition, his role as assistant helps him to see the problem from a completely different angle. The exercise is also beneficial to the therapeutic relationship because, for a few minutes, the two protagonists share an alliance as "experts."

Example 2
Co-Therapy with a Young Child

A 5-year-old child was referred to the school psychologist by his teacher. His parents were recently separated and he now lives alone with his father. For some time, the teacher has noticed a change in the pupil's behavior. He doesn't talk to the other children or even to his teacher. He is excessively distracted in class and seems to be increasingly closed in on himself. The school personnel suspect that he may be the victim of incest from his father.

_____

Therapist:

(*Considering the child's refusal to speak, the therapist decides not to directly question him but to pretend to amuse himself with a small red chair for children. Meanwhile, Felix is playing nearby and occasionally glances furtively at the therapist.*) Let's say that this chair is Felix (*as if talking to himself*). Oh! He doesn't talk much! (*Silence.*) He used to talk more. (*Silence.*) Now, he doesn't talk to anyone anymore…at least at school.

Felix:

(*Remains in his corner, watching what the therapist is doing from the corner of his eye.*)

Therapist:

(*Leaves long silences between his remarks, looking intensely at the little red chair and letting Felix play by himself in his corner.*) I don't know why he has become like this…the other kids would really like to be his friends…I think that Felix isn't very happy by himself…it's as if he is afraid of talking with others. Maybe that's because he has a secret he isn't supposed to tell.

Felix:
(*The rapid movements of Felix's eyes seem to indicate that the therapist has touched a sensitive point.*)

Therapist:
(*Treating the red chair tenderly and affectionately, as if the child were sitting in it. He pretends to gently touch his knees, hands, and head, and continues his monologue.*) I think that he must be very sad to keep it all inside…maybe he thinks that it's the best thing to do. But, if it's really the best solutions, why does it make him so sad? (*Silence.*) There must be another way to deal with things. (*Long silence, then takes out another little chair, white this time, and leans them against each other in a friendly way.*) Look at that! We'll say that this one is also Felix. He also has a secret…and he is afraid, very afraid to talk…(*silence.*) But he says, "If I never talk to any-one, I will be all alone with my problem, and I'll never have any friends! I will be afraid and cry every night. No! I don't want to! I don't like it!"

(*The therapist continues while Felix watches him furtively but attentively. The child can't resist because the therapist isn't addressing him directly. The therapist is only verbalizing different possibilities that are available to Felix to help the child think about the problem.*) And even if he is very, very afraid to talk about it, he decides anyway to do it…but to someone he can trust and who can help him. It has to be an adult, that's for sure. Do you see why? Look. (*The thera-pist is still talking to the small empty chair. He takes out a small bag with some objects in it.*) Do you see this bag? Let's say that it's like a 5- or 6-year-old child. Does a 5- or 6-year-old child know how to build a house all by himself? No. Does a 5- or 6-year-old child know his multipli-cation tables yet? Of course not. But he can get dressed by himself. He can write his name by himself. Of course he has some tools in his toolbag, but his bag isn't as big as an adult's toolbag. (*Takes out a big bag filled to capacity to symbolize an adult.*) That's why, if he talks about his secret to an adult, that adult can give him things that he hasn't even thought of yet because his bag is still too small. (*The therapist insists that the child needs to choose an adult as confidante to avoid the disappointment that would occur if he confided in a classmate.*) And, there are adults like me who are trained to help him.

I think that if he told his secret to at least one or two people, he wouldn't be so unhappy. At least he wouldn't have to be all alone with it. (*The therapist pretends to hold the hands of the child in the white chair while talking to him from very close by, with an inviting nonverbal attitude.*) If he told me, for example, since it's my work, I could suggest some ideas to him that would help him feel better, make friends again, and make everyone he loves happy (*referring to his father*)."

The method or "sales strategy" that the therapist is using is, in part, to describe the "what" the child is going through as precisely as possible and in simple language, in a way that the child can connect with and thus feel understood. In addition, the therapist attempts to describe solutions that the child has adopted to deal with the problem and any negative or costly consequences of his choice. The therapist then goes through the same exercise, showing the same situation after it has been solved using various options—such as talking with an adult who can help him—that give a much better result than in the first version.

The nonverbal language between the therapist and the small chairs lets the therapist work on the therapeutic relationship, even if the child refuses to participate. The therapist could then suggest to the child to keep one of the chairs, letting him choose the red one or the white one. Even if the child continues to be recalcitrant after watching the demonstration, the therapist can continue to help him, thanks to this approach. He also helps the child to dissociate from the problem despite himself, and to see it more objectively. He also shows the child a lot of affection and support through his verbal and nonverbal exchanges with the small chairs.

◎ Projection in Time

Edward Jacobs said in one of his seminars, "If we could make a person who is about to smoke his first cigarette feel, even for just 2 minutes, what it's like to have terminal lung cancer, with all the pain, powerlessness, and subjugation to medical treatments that come with it, he would probably never light up." This technique, which consists of projecting a situation over time, is in some ways an effort to create that type of amplified experience and prevent, in the present, problems that could develop in the future.

Example
Withdrawal after Becoming Handicapped

Joann was in a serious car accident and the surgeons had to amputate one leg to save her life. Two years later, Joann refuses to accept her disability and reintegrate into society. She spends most of her time sitting in front of the television, refusing all invitations and isolating herself as much as possible. Faced with this behavior, those close to her feel powerless and disconcerted, because they have always known her to be a dynamic, courageous, and determined woman. Eventually, Joann finds herself forced to consult a psychologist in order to maintain her disability insurance payments.

Therapist:
Joann, you live by yourself and spend all your time alone. Your brain gets its only stimulation from television and by thoughts of outrage, sadness, and powerlessness associated with your handicap. I'm guessing that your life, on a scale of 0 to 10, must be at about a 2, taking an optimistic view of things. Am I wrong?

Joann:
(*Does not answer, maintaining a distant attitude.*)

Therapist:
(*Places a chair behind the client.*) This chair represents Joann before she became disabled. She had two legs then. (*She writes "two legs" on a self-adhesive note and sticks it on to the chair behind Joann.*) I'm told she was dynamic, courageous, and determined (*writes those words on another note paper and sticks it onto the chair.*) Can you think of other remarkable characteristics she had?

Joann:
(*Is still silent, but appears to be thinking.*)

Therapist:
Was she sociable? Did she know how to surround herself with friends?

Joann:
(*Acquiesces, as if reliving that period of her life.*)

Therapist:
(*She writes down each of these characteristics and places the notes on the chair.*) Can you think of anything else that we can add to that chair to do justice to Joann?

Joann:
She loved kids a lot and always played with them, to spoil them, and get to know them better (*progressively sad and nostalgic*).

Therapist:
(*Adds that new aspect to the already well-decorated chair.*) Anything else?

Joann:

(*Indicates "no."*)

Therapist:

Very good. Now, let's take another chair. (*The therapist places it next to the client.*) Let's say that this is Joann right now. We know that the leg she lost in the accident has been replaced by a prosthesis (*she writes "one leg + one prosthesis" on a note and sticks it onto the new chair*). But tell me, which of Joann's characteristics should we transfer onto the new chair? Did the accident also amputate her courage and her love of children? Did the accident take away her determination? Or does she still have those old characteristics and is keeping them hidden inside her like prisoners? (*The therapist takes all the notes that were stuck to the "past" chair and places them in an envelope, closes it, and puts it on the "present" chair next to the client. The therapist lets Joann think about the question for a while before continuing, seeing that the client does not answer.*) There's also a chair that represents Joann in 5 years. (*She places another chair in front of the client.*) What shape do you think she will be in if she decides to keep the envelope closed until then?

Joann:

(*Cries bitterly for a while, then speaks between sobs.*) I can't live with just one leg. It's too hard….

Therapist:

That's not true; you can too live…but you need to go back to your envelope, open it, and keep all those notes in plain view. They belong to you. (*While speaking, she gives the envelope to the client and signals that she should open it.*)

Joann:

(*Contemplates the envelope for a long time, opens it, and lingers over each of the notes.*) It's weird…just holding this envelope and opening it makes me feel stronger already; more ready to become who…who…who I am, but with one leg less.

Therapist:

I think that for too long you've focused your attention on just one of those notes (*holds the note that says "one leg + one prosthesis" close to Joann's eyes, so that it hides the rest*) instead of seeing all of them (*puts the first paper back among the other notes that list her major characteristics*). What do you think?

Joann:

Yes!…that's exactly it!

Those little pieces of paper became very important in Joann's daily life, as well as in the sessions with her therapist that followed. She is never without them. The chair work allowed her to see the situation clearly and was a powerful driving force toward change.

◎ The Difference between Fantasy and Reality

Many unnecessary torments are due to overactive imaginations. If a child is 2 hours late getting home, the parents panic, imagining that he has been kidnapped. In fact, he's been having all kinds of fun with his friends and has simply forgotten the time. The boss is impatient because before leaving home he had a fight with his wife. The employee, seeing his boss's mood, is convinced that he is going to be fired, so he sleeps badly and has terrible indigestion for 3 days.

A useful exercise that can help these individuals distinguish between reality and their imagination is to take out two chairs, one of which is labeled "REALITY or 2+2=4" and the other label reads "IMAGINATION or 2+2=9." Begin by asking the client to sit in the first chair. The exercise consists of asking him to express the real facts concerning the problem in question. Next, the client sits in the other chair and reveals everything he imagined about the problem.

The therapist can use this exercise to help bring the client to understand the danger of sitting in the Imagination chair and the importance of sticking to the facts. He can also orient the exercise toward the development of communication skills to encourage the client to verify his hypothetical explanations in daily life.

◎ The Thinking Chair and the Parroting Chair

A technique that is somewhat similar to the previous one involves using two chairs, one of which "thinks" whereas the other does not. The first plays the role of the Adult (according to Transactional Analysis), the one who analyzes, evaluates, and is capable of honest judgment and decisions that favor his well-being. The chair that "doesn't think" represents the Critical Parent or the Adapted Child (also concepts from Transactional Analysis). These are dimensions of the ego that just repeat what they have heard or learned in childhood. They never judge the content of what they hear, but simply repeat it back like a parrot, day after day, year after year.

The experience of sitting in the two chairs and feeling and describing the cognitive and kinesthetic content really helps the client find the key elements he needs to make progress. The therapist can also help the client choose which chair he wants to use to lead his life, to determine which is the most successful, and to consider how to get rid of the other one. (This can include having the client take the chair out of the therapist's office.)

◎ Fear of Change

Have you had clients try to strike a bargain with you such as, "I want things to change but I don't want to change anything"? I suspect that many have been confronted more than once with this paradox. But how can we get a client to understand this internal contradiction when he is convinced that his position is coherent?

Example
Stacking Chairs

André is the king of liars. His mythomania has earned him frequent reprimands all during his childhood. From that experience he has understood that, if he pretends to agree, disagreements stop automatically. But that doesn't stop him from doing whatever he wants as soon as the occasion presents itself. At 42, his deceptions have become so substantial that he is now a prisoner of them. He says he wants to get out, but claims to be powerless to do so.

Therapist:

André, let me give you a demonstration of what is happening in our meetings since you started therapy with me. Let's say that the chair you are sitting on right now represents André in his present state, the one who lies daily.

That chair (*the therapist points to another chair that is a different style from the first one*) represents André who doesn't lie anymore, who has resolved to tell the truth, even if this is often difficult for him. Now, I'd like you to grab onto your chair and go sit down on the other one. (*This exercise often gives rise to some comical scenes. The client tries to sit on the second chair while holding the first one under him. Clearly, he quickly realizes that it is impossible to stack them.*)

André:

(*After a few fruitless attempts.*) It's impossible. This can't work!

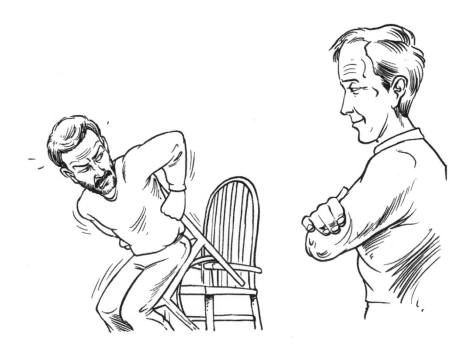

Therapist:
That's just what I thought! But don't you feel like that's what you've been trying to do for our last three meetings? (*The client suddenly realizes the meaning of the exercise.*) I think that the only way for you to feel better is to put aside your old behavior (*while speaking, the therapist leads André to let go of the first chair*) and to take the necessary steps to master a new way of dealing with differing opinions and arguments.

———————

Some clients will have an easier time understanding the process of change if we add a visual or kinesthetic dimension, as in this example. The participation of all the senses can leave a stronger and thus more useful impression.

It is advantageous to fully exploit the metaphor of the chairs to give maximal meaning to the exercise. The therapist should thus take the time needed to discuss the emotional and cognitive reactions of the client throughout the exercise. Did the client feel fear, lightness, or joy? Does he see obstacles to reaching the second chair? The therapist can include himself in the metaphor by giving a hand to the client to help him attain his goal. Does letting go of his old chair provoke any feelings of bereavement? In short, this exercise can help reveal abundant and varied information that is rich in pertinent content.

◎ Feeling Empty: Losing the Sense of Self

For 5 years, Denise, the only girl in her family, was sexually abused by her five brothers. Her only confidante was her diary. As she entered the house one day, she saw her father holding it. Her mother was standing next to him in tears. The reproving eyes of her father left no doubt that he had read the contents of the journal; he simply stared hard at his daughter before throwing the diary into the flames of the fireplace. Denise's mother was very retiring and submissive. Her brothers were excessively misogynistic, and her father was the president of that club. Denise was thus openly recognized by the family as responsible for the 5 years of sexual abuse.

Her brothers humiliated Denise at school, telling anyone within earshot that they had slept with her. Her father did not say a word to her for months at a time and began to be even closer to his sons. Through the years, her father's indifference and his vindictive mood were transformed into a sort of permanent punishment. Many years later, he transferred his successful business to his five sons.

At 40, Denise still has trouble paying her rent. Recently, she had proudly succeeded in buying a small new car, thinking she would amaze her father and brothers. Feeling superior in their latest luxury models, they only ridiculed her with all sorts of comments, refusing to even sit in her new acquisition. In addition, since she had left the family home, she had made it her duty to invite the family to dinner every Sunday in hopes of some day deserving a compliment or a thank you, for which she is still waiting.

After 30 years of vain efforts, ranging from bankruptcy to failures, she continues to stubbornly fight to regain the respect of her father and brothers. Her goal is not to do what pleases her, using all of her potential, but rather to impress the men in her family. Because they were the source of the denigrating messages about her, she mistakenly believes that they are the only ones who can change those messages.

In the face of the failure of all her efforts, she soothes her anger by stealing cheese from the grocery store. The depression surrounding her lack of success leads to evenings and entire nights in solitary tears. She constantly complains about headaches and obscure pains, and already has an impressive inventory of barbiturates to quiet the physical discomforts that remind her that "something is wrong." Her obsequious behavior with her family has also spread to the rest of her social interactions, so that she is completely overexploited. The more she steals, the more she cries and feels badly; the more she lets herself be exploited, the more she begins to believe that her father was right to call her a bad girl.

———————

Therapist:
What are your mother's, father's, and brothers' first names? (*As the client names them, the therapist writes them on self-adhesive notes and assigns each name to a chair. She places the seven chairs representing the two parents and the five brothers in a circle, while the client stands.*) Denise, sit here, please. Here is your brother, Bernard, the oldest. Put yourself in his place. I'd like you to tell me what you need to do to gain his respect.

Denise:
If I earned $150,000 to $200,000 a year, he would respect me more.

Therapist:
(*Wants to show that the client acts according to the expectations of others and not according to her own wishes, which is, in the opinion of the therapist, one of Denise's major problems.*) Are you doing something to try to attain that goal?

Denise:
(*Lets out a small exclamation of disgust.*) I've tried a lot of things. I can't count the times I've started a business or answered job advertisements for some stupid job that was supposed to pay $100,000 a year. But nothing has worked! Now I'm taking courses in marketing at the university. It's apparently a lucrative field.

Therapist:
How do you feel in that chair, Denise?

Denise:
(*Checks how she feels.*) As Bernard, I feel superior to Denise, stronger than her.

Therapist:
Does that feel pretty comfortable?

Denise:
Yes and no. His marriage failed and he doesn't see his kids anymore. His aggressiveness gets him in trouble a lot.

(*The therapist continues in this way with each of the people involved. The mother wants her daughter to keep quiet and conform, which Denise tries to do even if she sometimes feels like she is going to explode. Her father, now in a nursing home, demands that she call every day and come to see him once a week, as well as inviting him to dinner on Sundays. In addition, he uses emotional blackmail by suggesting that he might accept her more and maybe even compensate her financially when he dies if she follows his orders. One of her brothers had even implied that he would appreciate her more if she had a nice car. By using all her savings and then borrowing more money she was able to buy a car that clearly did not correspond to what he was thinking of. After making the tour of the family, the therapist took out a neutral chair and asked the client to sit in it.*)

Therapist:
What do you think of Denise's life?

Denise:
I understand why she might be confused!

Therapist:
And angry, sad, and lost?

Denise:
(*Tears come to her eyes as she sees all the roles she has tried to play for 30 years.*)

Therapist:

I think that there has always been one chair missing from this circle (*she places another chair in the circle and labels it "Denise"*). Would you like to try it?

Denise:

(*Exhibiting a mixture of pain and fatigue, Denise sits in the new chair and sobs silently.*)

Therapist:

(*After letting a long moment pass.*) What do you say from that position?

Denise:

(*Silence.*) I think that I've never really been here. I've always tried to satisfy everyone else. Not just my brothers and my parents, but everyone…I always thought that Denise's chair was terrible, wrong, bad, and awful. But now that I'm here, what I feel is the calm…the silence…the comfort of being at rest.

The staging organized by the therapist in this example could be developed, analyzed, and modified during three or four sessions or more, if necessary. All the elements are there to permit the client to get to the heart of the matter and to identify the physical sensations, emotions, and ideas that she needs to explore to make progress. The therapist can also have the client experience her relationship with each member of the family in different ways, by moving the chairs and role-playing, or provide specific training in assertiveness and communication, as needed.

◎ Distance

Impact Therapy is dedicated to keeping the client based in reality, or to bringing them back to it, whether that reality is positive or negative. What counts is to stay objective and realistic. Monique's problems started some time ago, dating from when her father left the family when she was only 6 years old. She says that she remembers running after him on the sidewalk and grabbing his leg to keep him from leaving, while he yelled at her, "Leave me alone, you are not my daughter!" even though he was her real father.

Some 25 years later, Monique keeps hoping for some sign from him. She writes to him each week, sends him a little money every month, and regularly gives him little gifts. Her father does not respond, does not thank her, and continues to ignore her as he has always done. Monique never accepted his leaving and keeps investing time and money in hopes of some day hearing an admission of love from her father. It is her dream, but she would be much better off if she kept to reality. Here is the staging that was set up to help her.

Therapist:
(*Places a chair as close as possible to the client's.*) Monique, I'd like you to imagine that this chair is your father's. He is close to you, listens to you, and is interested in your ideas, your projects, your work, and your life. He is encouraging, loving, helpful. He does all sorts of nice things for you, shows you love by calling you regularly and inviting you to his house occasionally. (*Overall, the therapist paints the idealized portrait of the father that Monique wishes so much to have.*)

Monique:
(*Crying with envy, frustration, and sadness as she listens to the description, imagining her father next to her, so supportive and protective, finally showing unconditional love for her.*)

Therapist:
That's really the father you'd like to have, isn't it?

Monique:
(*She nods, with the wide eyes of a dreamy child.*)

Therapist:
Now, Monique, I'd like you to show me where I should put your father's chair, so that it corresponds to his real position in your life.

Monique:

(*Snapping back to reality.*) There. No, a little further away.

Therapist:

(*She follows the client's instructions and places the chair at the other side of the room.*) Right now, Monique, is your father turned toward you or toward the door?

Monique:

(*Tired and sad*) Toward the door.

Therapist:

(*The therapist turns the chair toward the door.*) Has he ever been turned toward you in the last 25 years?

Monique:

(*Shakes her head while wiping away tears.*)

Therapist:

Does he get closer to you when you send him letters, money, and little gifts?

Monique:

(*Again reacts with sadness, recognizing that he still ignores her, no matter what she does.*)

Therapist:

Would you say that little Monique (*takes out a small child's chair to symbolize Monique when she was young*) believes that this man will become a good father if she does all she can to be a good girl?

Monique:

(*Begins to understand, with the help of the process of dissociation, that her dependence with regard to her father was coming from a part of herself.*) That's what I'm beginning to realize….

Therapist:

Do you think that she was right to believe that?

Monique:

No! Not only hasn't it worked for 25 years, but it seems as if the relationship has even gotten worse.

Therapist:

(*She places the small chair between the client and the father's chair to show that the little girl still controls the relationship.*) Do you still want to encourage her to keep investing in this relationship?

Monique:

No, I don't want to anymore.

Therapist:

I think that, in fact, he can't give her what she wants or respond to her requests. What would you say to playing that role in his place. (*As she speaks, she turns the small chair toward the client instead of toward the father. Suddenly Monique feels a wave of tenderness for the little girl. She understands that her responsibility is to nurture her and not to seek satisfaction from her father.*)

_____

Impact Techniques
Using Movements

C H A P T E R   3

It is known that human beings retain 70% of what they put into active practice and only 5% to 10% of what they hear. Curiously, despite knowing about this phenomenon, very few psychotherapeutic approaches that specifically attempt to create deep changes in the individual have incorporated these classic ideas to more effectively reach their clients. Maybe it is just a lack of inspiration. The following section suggests some solutions.

✳ The Child's Chair

In the previous chapter we saw many uses of the child's chair. Other effective applications that add the use of movements are also useful, or at least possible.

The child's chair can play the role of the inner Adapted Child—the one who causes problems, the one that carries all the defense mechanisms that are harmful to the balance and well-being of the individual (as conceptualized in Impact Therapy). Because of his immaturity, the Adapted Child often causes all sorts of conflicts in the various psychosocial spheres of the person's life, including in the family, at work or elsewhere. The small chair can thus be used to visualize the role of this part of the ego.

Example
A Couple under the Control of Their Adapted Child

Sean and Marie have always practiced the peculiar marital religion of mutually placing blame on the other person for even the most minor problems. After 15 years together, misunderstandings and resentment are omnipresent. They consult a psychotherapist to give their marriage one last chance.

The therapist needs to bring the clients to fully understand that the strategies they have been using during their disagreements originate from their earliest childhood. In addition to being completely ineffective, they are immature and obsolete. The therapist could start by taking out two small chairs to represent the Adapted Child part of each of them.

Therapist:
I'd like you to imagine yourselves sitting on these little chairs as children. (*By asking for descriptions of the young children—their haircuts, facial expressions, etc.—the therapist can accelerate and deepen the trance that links the two clients to their respective Adapted Child chairs.*) Tell me, what did you do to deal with things when something bothered you or when you were angry with someone?

Inevitably, the clients will describe the same means as those they still use and which are destroying their life as a couple: "I pouted," "I yelled," "I pretended I didn't care," "I made threats," "I found allies," and so on. Some of these strategies may have been camouflaged by pseudo-maturity, but don't be fooled: they are well and truly infantile tricks.

The use of methods that make the concepts concrete (by asking the clients to keep their Child chairs in front of them) rapidly leads the clients to insights about their life together. They both realize that their biggest problems come much more from their own little chair than from their partner's little chair. When they are asked to project themselves into the future and imagine what their lives would be like if they were not controlled by that part of themselves (by putting aside the small chairs that have separated them), an instantaneous relief and a new coming together of Adult and Adult comes into play. All these feelings reinforce the changes in their relationship in daily life. The sensations also let them rapidly identify any potential source of future conflicts.

Multiple messages are sent in this exercise. The most important is that which relates to the therapeutic contract. Each client arrived with the same request: change the other one. In the example above, the problem was redefined. It was no longer a question of the conflict between Sean and Marie, but rather one concerning the lack of control the two Adults had over the Adapted Children. Both of them have to work on themselves and to concentrate on their own evolution, instead of watching the attitudes and behavior of the other person with an eagle eye. This new task greatly enhances the revival of communication in the marriage and is a much more viable and beneficial project for therapy.

✖ Family Mediation

The two clients were fighting for custody of their 2-year-old son, Freddy, and did not care what weapons they used. To help them realize the toxic effects of their no-holds-barred approach, the therapist simply placed a small chair symbolizing Freddy between them and said, "Whoever deserves him most, take him!" (*indicating the small chair*). They both rushed to grab the chair so energetically that they almost completely demolished it. They were still tugging back and forth on it when the therapist said mildly, "How do you think your son feels right now?"

Thanks to this image of the virtually demolished little chair, they realized that Freddy was the real victim of their arguments. Thereafter, they completely modified their behavior.

✖ Sculpting

Sculpting was introduced to psychology by Virginia Satir (1967). Jacob Moreno (1964) also sometimes used similar techniques in his psychodramas, which were very popular among therapists for a time. The way sculpting is used in Impact Therapy is quite similar to the techniques elaborated by these two therapists, but some completely original elements have been added. The case descriptions that follow provide an array of ways to adapt these methods for use in evaluations and interventions.

Example 1
Father and Son

Mr. Downs and his son Marc, 19, arrive for their appointment. As is often the case with problems between two clients, each one tries to convince the therapist that the other person is wrong and should therefore change. Sculpting is a very useful tool because it asks each person to physically place themselves in terms of their specific position in the relationship. They can thus clearly see the distance they have moved in opposite directions. If one of the two has moved further from the starting point in the center of the room, the therapist cannot be accused of showing bias when describing the facts, because he is not the one who demonstrated the emotional distance in concrete terms.

_____

Therapist:

(*After a few moments of discussion.*) I think that we can save a lot of time if we do a brief exercise. (*He gets up and asks the son to do the same. They move to the center of the room. The father remains seated.*) Usually, in a relationship where everything is going fine, the two people stand side by side or even hold hands, which shows that they feel good with regard to other person. (*In this case, because there is a great deal of tension between the two clients, the therapist plays the father's role and takes Marc's hand, to avoid forcing the two men to hold hands. Note that the therapist makes a very brief presentation.*) In your case, the situation is different. You're here precisely because your relationship in not going well. In a second, I will ask you to place yourselves with respect to the other person (*signals the father to rise*). Simply act in the way that seems the most natural. One, two, three. (*The father moves as far away as possible from his son and turns his back on him. For his part, Marc takes two or three steps back, but remains turned toward his father.*)

(*The evidence shows that to solve their problems, Mr. Downs has more steps to take than his son. He is more distant and withdrawn than his son, whereas Marc seems more inclined to collaborate.*

It is difficult to explain this type of interpretation of a relationship to a recalcitrant client on the basis of a verbal evaluation alone. He may well deny everything, perhaps insult the therapist or accuse him of taking sides with the other party. Such strong reactions can seriously compromise the possibility of progress. On the other hand, if the evaluation is conducted judiciously using sculpting, it provides physical evidence that the clients themselves both demonstrate and feel. Consequently, it is much easier for them to accept the therapist's comments and analysis.)

Therapist:
What do you notice about this exercise?

Mr. Downs:

Personally, I've already done a lot! I've done everything for that kid. Now it's gotten to the point where I don't want to do anything anymore. It would do no good anyway.

Therapist:

And you, Marc?

Marc:

I don't agree. If only, instead of closing himself off, he would agree to talk! I'm ready to respect his needs, but I wish that mine were also respected. We could make a compromise.

Therapist:

Looking at what you've shown me with this exercise, it seems clear to me that, you, Mr. Downs, feel very hurt and perhaps also disappointed by all the efforts that you've already made that appear to have been useless. But, if you really want to give the relationship another chance, you will have to be ready to invest in it again. Then we'll look at the stages that you will move through progressively to improve the situation.

———————

No matter how the participants react, the therapist can always use the results of the sculpting to confirm his diagnosis and the process that will be necessary for each individual to go through in order to reach their common goal of an improved relationship. In this way, the therapist remains in a position of neutrality while still asking more from one of the clients.

Example 2
The Required Interdependence in Marital Therapy

The sculpting exercise can also be used in interventions with couples. In such cases, the man and woman are each asked to "sculpt" themselves in relation to each other.

Therapists must often consider how to seat the man and woman for a couple's therapy session. Should you place them close to each other, slightly separated, or completely apart? Sculpting allows a couple to demonstrate the state of their emotional relationship in physical and spatial terms.

Often the two protagonists come to therapy after being subjected to each other's wrath. Thus, they are both feeling hurt, sometimes afraid, or resigned to losing the relationship. In this situation, they tend to put a lot of distance between them. Often, their paths from the center of the room will literally lead them in opposite directions.

The first goal is to make them aware of the opposition between the goal of therapy (to give their relationship a last chance) and their current path (heading in opposite directions, at least as indicated by where they placed themselves in the exercise). Using sculpting, it is much easier to bring them to turn toward each other and to realize that they will need to make real efforts for the survival of their marriage. Both the visual representation of their relative positions and the very strong emotions inherent in this technique, will help bring them to understand that they will need to proceed step by step to come together again. The therapist can describe each of the required steps according to his or her school of thought.

In my sessions, I lead the couple through four stages (which are also useful for any conflictual interpersonal relationship, such as parent-child, brother-sister, employer-employee, etc.). The first stage is called the cease fire: to me, it seems difficult to reconstruct something without having first interrupted the war. The second stage is aimed at bringing the two clients to recognize their full responsibility in the degeneration of the conflict. In general, the memory of a fight in which each had volubly raised the stakes with escalating arguments is enough to show that blame is shared by both sides.

Once these steps have been taken, it is easier to introduce the principles of communication and conflict resolution (or problem solving) before proceeding to the last stage, which is to nurture the relationship by incorporating gestures of caring that each party offers the other. This stage differs from the previous one in the sense that it goes beyond just words.

No matter what theoretical framework guides your interventions with troubled relationships, it is always advantageous to guide clients to take actual steps measure for measure with the description of the stages of therapy. In this way, they will understand that they will have to change directions, move and make progress, and no one can do it in their place. The only way to help them free themselves of the anger they have inside is to bring each to look at himself instead of judging the other. This new point of view gives both of them the power to change their situation.

Coat Rack

In their roles as mothers, our grandmothers worked relentlessly to assure the well-being of their families. Times have changed, but the women of today still find themselves carrying a heavy load: to excel as professionals while being devoted and irreproachable at home. Very often, there comes a time when the demands of her multiple roles take on invasive proportions. The mother then brings the members of her family to therapy so that they will learn to appreciate and respect her. But, curiously, we often see that the mother herself perpetuates the situation that she condemns. In the case presented below, the problem had degenerated to the point where the children and the father did not dare come in the house for fear of hearing the familiar litany of complaints from Amanda.

Therapist:

(*Addressing the children and father.*) I want to suggest an exercise that will let everyone better understand the uncomfortable situation at your house. I'd like each of you to find three or four objects in this room that can represent the demands you make on Amanda each week. And Amanda, I'd like you to also find a few objects to represent your personal pastimes or those you would like to have, and another to symbolize your work (*everyone does what was asked and explains to the others the meaning of the chosen objects*). Now, I will count to three and I

want each of you to give Amanda, all at the same time, the objects you have while making your requests as you would ordinarily do.

(The father and the three children move together toward the mother, some more quickly than others. One person makes polite requests, another one makes demands, and a third negotiates. Each one uses their natural style to get what they want. Amanda agrees to all their demands, but not without complaining. After a moment, she finds herself with objects hanging all over her, trying without complete success to hold on to all of them without letting anything fall. She resembles an overloaded coat rack.)

Therapist:

I'd first like to ask you, what did you get out of this exercise?

Oldest child:

I thought that my two or three demands weren't such a big deal, but I realize that everyone else is coming with the same type of request and Mom has to satisfy everyone.

Another child:

I understand why she's always complaining!

Father:

Can we help her out with this stuff now?

Therapist:

That depends on what you want to take back from her.

Father:

(Realizes that it's not just a game and that he will be expected to take responsibility in daily life for the things that he takes back in the exercise.) I can't do my mending, but I can make my own lunches *(he gets up to relieve his wife of the object representing lunches but finds the therapist blocking his way.)*

Therapist:

You're sure you want to take back that one? That means that, from now on, every evening, you will spend some time preparing your lunch for the next day. You realize that, right?

(The therapist continues, leading each child and the father to take responsibility for their actions. After a while, Amanda begins to emerge from the pile of "demands" and takes on her share of responsibility in the family dynamic.)

Amanda:

No, I can do the laundry and make dinner. That doesn't bother me. (*She had already refused to give up doing the grocery shopping, the budget, and birthday parties.*)

Therapist:

Amanda, I notice that the others have offered to help you with a number of tasks and you have refused. Do you think that attitude might have contributed in part to the problem?

Amanda:

(*Accepting responsibility for her part in the established dynamic.*) I think you're right!

_____

The demonstration of the "coat rack" is a perfect way to represent the situation in which many overloaded mothers, secretaries, managers, bosses—and even some therapists—find themselves.

✖ Continuum

The continuum, which represents the path to be traveled, is equally useful in individual, marital, family, and group interventions. It takes only a few seconds to do and what it reveals can be the basis for discussion and further exploration for an entire therapy session.

Example 1
Unfocused Client

Sometimes, the beginning of a session seems to drag out without ever really getting started. The client flits from one minor innocuous detail of his week to another, leading himself and the therapist completely off track. The hour is over with no progress having been made on the real problem. Think I'm exaggerating? Then you are one of the fortunate few!

Nonetheless, just in case this situation arises, it is useful to have an effective tool to help get our most loquacious clients onto the right track and to do so in the first few minutes of the session.

One excellent way of doing this is to ask the client to stand with his back to the wall on the far side of the room (this works even if you have a small office).

Therapist:

Jenny, the place where you're standing represents the starting point in your therapy. The wall on the other side of the room represents your goals, the things that you want to accomplish in therapy. Could you show me how far along you are today?

This simple exercise helps the client to rediscover her motives for consulting a therapist and, in future sessions, she can use the same physical metaphor to show her progress. The therapist could ask the client for details about what has been accomplished, to help consolidate the progress. In the same way, the client and therapist can discuss the next steps that need to be taken toward the ultimate goal. This way, both client and therapist can stay on track.

Example 2
Stalled Progress

Many other possible applications of the continuum can be added to the situation discussed above. For example, clients whose progress stalls can be greatly helped using this technique. Once such a client has shown his progress by placing himself somewhere between the starting point and the goal, the therapist can ask how long he has been at the same place.

Hugh:

That's a good question! (*Thinks about it.*) I would say about 3 weeks.

Therapist:

That's about what I thought, too. Do you have the feeling that, for the last 3 weeks, you've been moving like this (*the therapist stands near Hugh and moves from side to side*), without going forward or backwards, but talking about all kinds of side issues?

Hugh:

Yes, that's exactly what's been happening!

Therapist:

Hugh, have you noticed that our relationship has deteriorated in the last 3 weeks?

Hugh:

(*A little embarrassed to admit it.*) Yeah.

Therapist:

I've been asking myself why. Things were going well and then…I think that this might be because I've been pulling you forward, to try to respect the commitment we made at the beginning—that is, to help you better understand your relationship with your father. But meanwhile, you've been pulling me sideways by talking about your friends! Couldn't that be the cause of the tension between us?

Hugh:

(*Appears satisfied with that explanation.*) It makes sense.

Therapist:

So, what should we do? Do you want us to renegotiate our agreement or do you want to pursue the goals we already established?

Hugh:

(*Enthusiastically.*) I agree that we should continue working on the original goal.

Example 3
Ending the Therapeutic Process

The connection created between a client and her therapist sometimes comes to feel like a nice home that is difficult to leave. The continuum has helped me more than once prepare a client for the end of therapy. As in the previous example, the client places himself to indicate his progress on the continuum. When he finds himself at the end, the image will stay in his mind until his next appointment—which often proves to be his last.

One day, one of my clients said, "Here I am (*just one small step from the goal*), but I'm like this (*turning back toward the starting point*)!" Wasn't that eloquent? And it led to an interesting discussion.

Example 4
Smart Choices

This technique can be used whenever the client is facing a major decision: to keep a baby or place it for adoption, stay married or get divorced, and so on. Each wall of the office is used to represent an option, creating four directions the client can move. The client begins the exercise in the middle of the room and should then place herself so as to indicate her position at the time of the appointment. We can also ask her to show which direction she is heading. By experiencing different positions relative to the possible choices, important elements may emerge that may help guide her decision.

For career counseling, the four walls may represent four different career options. An exploration of the multiple possible trajectories can save a lot of time in evaluating those options. On the one hand, they provide a visual representation and, on the other hand, they force the client to stay focused on the subject under discussion and to report any significant thoughts or feelings.

Example 5
Taking Stock of One's Professional Life

To evaluate your professional life, you can stand with your back toward one wall (you can do this right now, if you wish). The wall across the room represents having reached all your goals and the wall behind you symbolizes the beginning of your efforts to reach those goals. Now, move along that continuum so that your position represents, as honestly as possible, your current situation. Once you have done that, put one foot in front of the other and ask yourself what your next step toward your professional goals should be. When will you take that step? How will you feel after you take it? (Physically take that step to put yourself in that position.)

Some people will spontaneously feel the need to change the basic premise of this exercise (this may also be true in the previous examples). I remember a woman who, after working as a secretary in a school for 18 years, decided to become a social worker. She did not hesitate to designate two continuums rather than just one. She had already followed the first to the very end, whereas she has barely started on the second. Such adaptations can only enrich the exercise.

Example 6
School Dropout

Clients often find themselves at a crossroad. Adolescents, especially those headed toward a dead end, can be helped with greater efficacy if their reality is represented in concrete terms.

_____

Therapist:

Judith, I'd like you to stand here, in the center of the room. You have many options. Let's say that this one (*indicating a direction*) represents dropping out and that one (*indicating the opposite direction*) represents continuing in school. If you follow the first, where do you think that will lead you?

Judith:

I don't know. I just want to be done with courses, homework, and teachers!

Therapist:

But where will that lead you? Shouldn't we ask that question? It's essential to know whether your choice will make your position worse, isn't it?

Judith:

It can't be worse than it is now.

Therapist:

I think that probably the first steps along that path, of dropping out, seem more tolerable than the other path. But what do you make out if you look halfway down and to the end of that path?

Judith:

It's like I'd rather not see.

Therapist: (*Takes out a pair of glasses with completely opaque lenses. She asks Judith to put them on and continue along the "dropout" path.*) So, this is what you just told me. Do you prefer not seeing what you're heading for?

Judith:

(*Stops moving.*) Yeah, well. That wasn't a very good idea.

Therapist:

And if you look in the other direction, where do you think that path will lead you?

Judith:

It makes me sick to stay in school!

Therapist:

Ah! You see? It's the inverse of the other situation. This time, the first part seems terrible to you, but if you look further, what do you see?

Judith:

I don't know if I can get past the first part!

Therapist:

If the rest of the path interests you, there is always a way of finding assistance to help you succeed in getting through the tough parts!

Many variations of this type of movement can be added to the demonstration described in this example to improve the experience. Let your imagination run wild!

Refusal to Collaborate

The following example concerns a 14-year-old who doesn't seem to want to be helped by the therapist. After three appointments, the adolescent scorned all the therapeutic contracts that the therapist had offered. In fact, he seemed determined to maintain an attitude of closed politeness. He appeared to want to satisfy his need for vengeance against his mother, by making her uselessly pay for his therapy sessions every week.

Therapist:

Alex, today our session will last 5 minutes and it will be free. (*The client looks completely surprised.*) We've seen each other three times and, at every appointment, I have offered you my help. (*The therapist is seated next to Alex and offers him his hands to visually demonstrate what he is expressing.*) I offered you my help to improve your grades, which are in free fall. Not only did you reject the offer, but you attacked it. (*Extends his hands toward the client and asks Alex to strike them. He then presents his hands again to show that, in spite of Alex's reaction, he persisted in making the offer.*) Then, I offered to help you with your stuttering. Again, you refused. (*The therapist again signals the client to strike his hands. The therapist continues to enumerate the various contracts that he tried in vain to establish with Alex. Each time, he asks the client to hit his hands to indicate that it is the client, not the therapist, who is the principal architect of his current fairly miserable situation.)*

Alex:

Hey man! Don't take it personally!

Therapist:

I don't feel personally attacked, Alex. But, after our three appointments together, my conclusion is that you are at about a 2 on a scale of 10. Your grades keep going down. You don't have any friends. You spend your evenings alone in your room. Your stuttering and your acne are getting worse by the day and you approach the world with anger and revulsion that you don't hide or control very effectively. I think that you need help and that you could make use of that help to feel better. I'll leave you with those thoughts, Alex, and if you ever decide to accept a helping hand, I'll still be here (*the therapist once again extends his hands toward the client*). But, the next time, I want it to be you who contacts me, not your mother.

———————

The client was fairly stunned by this intervention. It took 5 months before he called, but this time he really wanted to be helped.

I think that many clients keep going to therapy, even though they are getting absolutely nothing out of it. Even worse, they go around loudly telling people that they were in therapy for a year and it did not help at all. With clients like these, the task of any future therapist will be doubly hard. He would first have to convince them that there is still hope and that it is possible to overcome their difficulties.

I dream of being able to use this technique with elderly individuals who have been placed in nursing homes against their will and who refuse to leave their rooms or get to know the other residents. In so doing, they diminish their own lives until they are completely miserable. Like Alex, they refuse any help that is offered. Perhaps this type of intervention could help them realize the active role they play in creating the desolation in which they are living.

❊ The Corner

The corner technique is used to address problems of depression and suicidal ideation. One common denominator of these diagnoses is very likely a distancing from the self, from their own needs and aspirations. The example below concerns a suicidal client.

Therapist:

(*Seeing that an immediate positive impact during the session is needed to avoid hospitalization.*) Helen, I'd like you to stand in the corner of the room.

Helen:

(*Responds to the request and places herself with her back to the corner.*)

Therapist:

I'd like you to face the corner, please. Now, move forward as much as possible.

Helen:

(*Moves into the corner until her feet, her body and her head cannot go any further.*)

Therapist:

How do feel there in the corner, Helen?

Helen:

(*Takes a few seconds to notice what she is experiencing.*) I feel alone. (*Becomes more and more attentive to her inner world.*) I can't catch my breath...I'm getting a headache from pushing....it's dark...I'm sad because I feel like, no matter how much energy I put into trying to move forward, I'll never be able to....

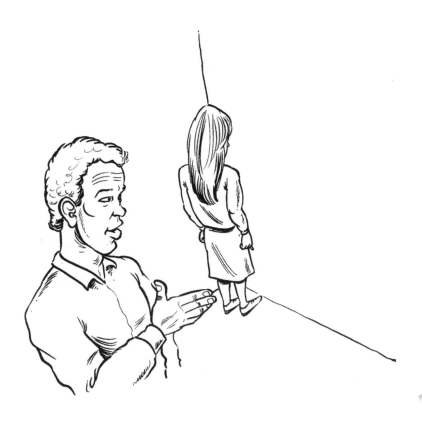

Therapist:

Is that sort of how you feel in everyday life?

Helen:

(*Dejected.*) Yes…a lot.

Therapist:

I think that it is, in fact, exactly what's happening to you. You've been moving in the same direction forever, which has finally led you to an impasse. Your philosophy is to not say what you think, not listen to your needs, not share your opinions, and go along with the crowd instead of listening to yourself. Helen, anyone who follows that direction would end up in the same place. I don't know who gave you these ideas, but they definitely aren't getting you where you want to go. Do you have any ideas of how you can get out of there?

Helen:

I don't know…but it seems that if I look between my feet, I can see light!

Therapist:

That's exactly the direction I was going to suggest: 180 degrees opposite of where you're heading now. In other words, start to express your thoughts; to listen to and respect your ideas and your needs; to believe in your aspirations. Make a quarter-turn toward me now. (*The client turns a bit.*) How do you feel in that position?

Helen:

It's better. There's a little more air and I can breathe better. I can also see light. I don't feel so much like a prisoner.

Therapist:

Turn a little bit more. What's your reaction now?

Helen:

It's weird. I felt a kind of release. I have the feeling that I'm discovering life like a child would!

Therapist:

Take a little step forward then.

Helen:

(*Follows the therapist's instructions.*) That scares me.

Therapist:

Welcome to the club! It's normal to be afraid every time we try something new. It's even worse when it comes to saying what we think or what we feel. On the other hand, do you realize that this is the only way to leave your suffering behind?

———————

This experience helped the client understand that there were alternatives to suicide. It also showed her how to take her place as the leading actress in her own life and to understand that she had the power to radically modify her situation. The exercise not only provided an etiologic explanation of the problem, but also offered a solution.

✴ Change in Therapy

Strangely, many clients believe that the simple fact of coming and sitting for an hour a week in their therapist's office will automatically transform their lives and that, in addition, the change will happen all by itself. Very few among them realize that they need to change something if they want their life to be more satisfying. When this type of attitude is suspected, it is better to try to make the client aware of it rather than waiting for them to realize it on his own.

———————

Therapist:

Ben, let me explain something to you. Do you see that chair? Let's say that it represents everything that dissatisfies you. That other chair (*the therapist strategically chooses the chair that is farthest away*) represents what you are looking for—a more satisfying and tranquil life. I'm going to ask you sit in the first one (*which the client does*) and to tell me where you are in your path toward your goal (*points to the other chair*).

Ben:

(*Seems to find the question very pertinent, but has to admit that he hasn't made any progress at all.*) I think I'm still here.

Therapist:

That's what I thought, too. How can you explain that?

Ben:

Well, I haven't felt any changes yet.

Therapist:

How do you think you are going to get to the other chair?

Ben:

(*Thinks a while.*) When I understand all about my past?

Therapist:

There you are! I think that's the problem. I think, Ben, that the only way to reach our goals is, first of all, to get up. (*The therapist asks Ben to follow his instructions.*) That means that you are really ready to change your behaviors and your reactions in order to create a more satisfying life. Next, a few steps forward are needed, which means that you need to concretely start to do things differently when dealing with situations and people. This might sometimes be frightening, but unfortunately I don't know of any other way of doing it. Then, you can sit in the other chair and calmly get used to its comfort and to the new perspective you will have from there (*the client physically does what the therapist says during the entire explanation*). I'm only here as a guide to give you a hand in case you ever trip along the way.

Ben:

I hadn't understood that part of things before. I already feel as if, today, I'll make more progress than I did before. I understand better what I have to do now.

✳ Maslow's Hierarchy

This is a classic. Many clients find themselves unable to progress through all the levels of Maslow's hierarchy (Maslow, 1954). This theory describes the development of the personality as occurring through the satisfaction of various needs in a hierarchical fashion:

- Physiological needs (thirst, hunger, sleep, bodily needs, sexuality, etc.)
- Need for security (physical protection)
- Need for love and belonging (affiliation and acceptance)
- Need for esteem (success, recognition, status)
- Need for self-actualization (personal fulfillment, self-realization)

The hierarchical principle dictates that the needs of the lower level must be met before being able to reach the next level. Thus, many people find themselves stuck at the level of needing love and belonging, and can never gain access to the level of esteem or full self-actualization. (For those who are not familiar with these theories, reading more about them is highly recommended before applying these ideas.)

In clinical use, the five levels are written on separate sheets of papers and placed about two feet apart along a straight line. Each level is briefly explained to the client and he is asked to place himself, relative to the five levels, where he was at different times of his life.

Therapist:
I'm going to ask you to show me where you were on this scale when you were 3 years old.

Client:
When I was 3, I was here, at the need for love and belonging. I did everything according to what others wanted, so that they would love and accept me.

Therapist:
And now?

Client:
(*Thinks briefly.*) I think that I'm still there, but maybe one step forward, toward the need for esteem! I want to pursue my studies, but I haven't really put all my energy into it because my husband says he doesn't understand me anymore. Both of us think that, if I get too far ahead of him, it will destroy our relationship.

Therapist:

Could you show me where your husband is on this scale?

Client:

I suspect he is more at the level of the need for security. He's very worried about our financial situation, especially about our retirement. I think that he wrongly thinks that we don't have enough money and he would like to save more and limit our expenses as much as possible. Of course, that would include me dropping my studies!

Therapist:

How would you demonstrate the dynamic of your relationship using this scale?

Client:

I can see now what is happening. It seems to me that he doesn't understand my need for esteem and self-fulfillment at all. He would like me to return to the need for security and stay there. (*Silence as she thinks deeply.*) But I refuse to go backwards. I want to keep moving forward and I'm afraid he'll just have to follow me or stay there moping in front of his bank statement.

This demonstration allows the client to develop a new understanding of her situation and to clarify her needs.

✳ Obstacles

Very often, clients do not make progress toward their goals because of various obstacles. An image of the hoped-for situation can be very profitable. The use of various objects (chairs, tables, lamps, wastebaskets, etc.) can help to concretely represent the various traps that can appear along the client's path.

Therapist:

Jack, here are the goals you want to reach. (*The therapist has simply written the goals on sheets of paper that he has attached to the wall.*) I will place some obstacles between you and your goals. Together, we will then try to name what they could represent and to determine how you can get rid of them, avoid them, or overcome them.

This simple dramatization helps lead the client to face his problems and to stay focused on the subject during the entire session. The therapist can make this experience even more fruitful by coming back to it as needed in later sessions.

✳ To Clarify a Situation

I strongly believe in staging of the client's situation to make new significant information emerge, as much for the client as for the therapist. One day, a therapist was desperate because he had not been able to help a client who was really not making progress. The 19-year-old client seemed to have decided to take drugs and hang out in suspect and dangerous bars for the rest of his life. He had dropped out of school, sold pot, lived at night, and loved his long ponytail and his multiple bracelets. Summer and winter, he dressed in black t-shirts and shorts, black socks, and combat boots. The therapist had nonetheless developed a very good relationship with Philip and believed in him until…finally he really began to have serious doubts! As a last resort, he tried to demonstrate the situation.

Therapist:

Philip, I'd like to try to stage what is happening in your life right now, okay?

Philip:

Sure. Go for it!

Therapist:

Let's say that the wall behind you represents the school. The wall in front of you represents drugs, and everything that is marginal and illegal. I'll play your father, who is trying to push you toward school. (*His father gave him a lot of grief about this issue. Note that the therapist does not tell the client how to react. The power of this technique comes precisely from the fact that the client behaves completely naturally, revealing important information. The therapist begins to gently push Philip toward the school. Philip strongly opposes this and pushes so hard that they both find themselves close to the "drug" wall, which is where the exercise ended.*)

Therapist:

Philip, don't you see that you're about to go over the edge? If the first wall (*the "school" wall*) is a big zero for you, that one (*indicating the "drug" wall*) is just as bad! Why do you want to go there?

Philip:

I don't *want* to go there! I'm simply avoiding going to school!

Without even realizing it, Philip was using a force diametrically opposed to his father's (physics textbooks clearly say that for every action there is an equal and opposite reaction). However, since he pushed back a little bit harder than his father, he kept moving toward drugs.

The exercise helped Philip. He realized for himself that he was in the process of "being had" in his own game and that he was moving in a direction he had not chosen. For the therapist, the concrete demonstration put an end to his suspicions about his client. Thereafter, they worked together to find other ways of dealing with his father and other more enriching directions to explore. Philip registered at a music school, got his sky-diving certificate, and, the last we heard, had just come back from 3 months in Australia where he had worked on various fruit and vegetable farms to earn a little money while exploring another part of the world.

To stage a client's reality, one simply has to think in terms of images: How can I illustrate how he functions with regard to his problems or his life in general and reproduce it as closely as possible?

In passing, the best way to use this approach with clients is first to make a list of your regular clients (or, for those who only do evaluations, a list of the problems you commonly encounter) and to find images to describe them. One can then begin to practice staging, beginning with the clients whose problems are most easily represented in concrete terms. You'll very rapidly find yourself at ease with this type of intervention.

✖ Going in Circles

People have all kinds of ways of expressing what they are going through. If we know how to listen, we can make good use of their descriptions. Frank said he had been going in circles for several months. The therapist took him at his word.

Therapist:

Frank, before going on with our discussion, I would like to get up and start to go in circles while we continue to talk.

Frank:

What?

Therapist:

(*Gets up and starts walking in a circle and invites the client to follow him.*) How do you feel, Frank?

Frank:

I feel like I'm going nowhere!

Therapist:

Do you feel a sense of well-being, heaviness, lightness…?

Frank:

No, more like weariness, boredom.

Therapist:

Has it occurred to you to leave the circle? (*All of this is happening while the two walk in a circle.*)

Frank:

I'm afraid just thinking of it. I'm only 20, I dropped out of school just 2 years ago and I'm already afraid that I can't learn anymore.

The therapist's questions solicit much more detail if the client is living his normal life experience during the discussion. Possible solutions can also be explored and consolidated in the same context. In the case above, Frank physically left the circle to go explore another corner of the office and came back to his original position to describe his impressions. The exercise generally proves much more effective than if the discussion is limited to strictly verbal exchanges.

Conclusion

My most ardent wish is that this book has let you understand the heart of Impact Therapy. It is not a question of techniques alone, it is a question of attitude: an attitude that reflects authenticity, courage, and simplicity, and which is based on knowledge of and respect for human functioning. I frequently meet colleagues who are on the verge of leaving the profession because they have not found a way to express their vision and their identity within it. In adopting a position of neutrality, they had forgotten themselves. Impact Therapy makes use of the therapist's individuality, emotions, and creativity. I am not simply a therapist. I am an individual: I am Danie, or Richard, or Sandra, etc. I am not just a sympathetic listening ear. I am an ally, an experienced collaborator, wise and inventive.

On the other hand, if this approach offered nothing but definitive answers, it would rapidly become dogmatic and in so doing lose its capacity to self-correct and evolve. There is still much to discover in psychotherapy in order to make treatments even more effective and rapid. It is thus important to stay on the lookout for anything that might enrich our clinical knowledge.

Writing a book, regularly working on it over a long period of time, can lead to a sort of near-sightedness. By concentrating on the details, the author sometimes loses sight of general principles. To improve future volumes, I would appreciate receiving your comments, suggestions, and the results of your experimentation with these techniques, and I thank you in advance for your collaboration.

I conclude with these words from Richard Bandler, a clinician who I appreciate very much for his lucidity:

> *There is a huge difference between learning some things, and discovering what there is still to learn. That is the difference that makes the difference.*

References

Berne, E. (1964). *Games people play*. New York: Grove Press.

Bottini, G., Corcoran, R., Sterzi, R., et al. (1994). The role of the right hemisphere in the interpretation of figurative aspects of language. A positron emission tomography activation study. *Brain, 117*(6), 1241-1253.

Brownell, H. H., Simpson, T. L., Bihrle, A. M., et al. (1990). Appreciation of metaphoric alternative word meanings by left and right brain-damaged patients. *Neuropsychologia, 28*(4), 375-383.

Calvert, G., Brammer, M., Bullmore, E., et al. (1999). Response amplification in sensory-specific cortices during crossmodal binding. *Neuroreport, 10*(12), 2619-2623.

Calvert, G., Campbell, R., & Brammer, M. (2000). Evidence from functional magnetic resonance imaging of crossmodal binding in the human heteromodal cortex. *Current Biology, 10*(11), 649-657.

Calvert, G., Hansen, P., Iversen, S., & Brammer, M. (2001). Detection of audio-visual integration sites in humans by application of electrophysiological criteria to the BOLD effect. *NeuroImage, 1* (2), 427-438.

Calvert, G. A. (2001). Crossmodal processing in the human brain: Insights from functional neuroimaging studies. *Cerebral Cortex , 11*(12), 1110.

Faust, M., & Weisper, S. (2000). Understanding metaphoric sentences in the two cerebral hemispheres. *Brain Cognition, 43*(1-3), 186-191.

Goulding, R., & Goulding, M. (1978). *The power is in the patient. A TA/Gestalt approach to psychotherapy*. San Francisco: TA Press.

Grady , C. L., McIntosh, A. R., Rajah, M. N., & Craik, F. I. M. (1997). Neural correlates of the episodic encoding of pictures and words. *Proceedings of the National Academy of Sciences of the United States of America, 95*(5), 2703-2708.

Isnard, G. (1990). *L'enfant et sa mémoire*. France: Mercure de France.

Jacobs, E. E. (1992). *Creative counseling techniques: An illustrated guide*. Minneapolis: Educational Media Corporation.

Jacobs, E. E. (1994). *Impact therapy*. Odessa, FL: Psychological Assessment Resources.

James, M., & Jongerald, D. (1978). *Naître gagnant*. Paris: InterÉditions.

Kotler, P. (2003). *Marketing insights from A to Z*. New York: Wiley & Sons.

Moreno, J. L. (1964). *The first psychodramatic family.* New York: Beacon House.

Maslow, A. (1954). *Motivation and personality.* New York: Harper.

Rosen, S. (1991). *My voice will go with you: The teaching tales of Milton H. Erickson, M.D.* New York: Norton.

Satir, V. (1967). *Conjoint family therapy; a guide to theory and technique.* Palo Alto, CA: Science and Behavior Books.

Smith, Hy. (1996) *Mes valeurs, mon temps, ma vie.* Montréal: Un Monde Différent.

Trout, J., & Steve, R. (1998). *The power of simplicity: Management guide to cutting through the nonsense.* New York: McGraw-Hill Ryerson Limited.

Books by the Same Author

Beaulieu, D. (2005). *L'intégration par les mouvements oculaires*. France: Éditions Le Souffle d'Or.

———. (2004). *Impact techniques in the classroom: 88 activities to engage your students*. Wales, UK: Crown House Publishing.

———. (2003). *Eye movement integration therapy*. Wales, UK: Crown House Publishing.

———. (2002). *Fascicules d'impact en classe: Activités éducatives pour développer toutes les intelligences* (9 numéros). Québec: Éditions Académie Impact.

———. (2001). *Techniques d'impact en classe*. Québec: Éditions Académie Impact.

———. (2000). *Techniques d'impact pour grandir: Illustrations pour développer l'intelligence émotionnelle chez les enfants*. Québec: Éditions Académie Impact.

———. (2000). *Techniques d'impact pour grandir: Illustrations pour développer l'intelligence émotionnelle chez les adolescents*. Québec: Éditions Académie Impact.

———. (2000). *Techniques d'impact pour grandir: Illustrations pour développer l'intelligence émotionnelle chez les adultes*. Québec: Éditions Académie Impact.

———. (2000). *Cures de rajeunissement pour vos relations sexuelles*. Québec: Éditions Académie Impact.

———. (1999). *100 trucs pour améliorer vos relations avec les enfants*. Québec: Éditions Académie Impact.

———. (1997). *100 trucs pour améliorer vos relations avec les ados*. Québec: Éditions Académie Impact.

Roy, É., & Beaulieu, D. (2003). *Techniques d'impact au préscolaire*. Québec: Éditions Académie Impact.

About the Author

Danie Beaulieu, Ph.D., holds a doctorate in psychology from the University of Montreal and is a trained hypnotherapist. She is the only certified instructor of Impact Therapy in Canada and the only psychotherapist in Canada authorized to teach Eye Movement Integration (EMI) therapy for the treatment of post-traumatic stress syndromes.

Her passion for psychology in all its forms is contagious: a respected and sought-after speaker in Quebec, she gives an ever-increasing number of presentations as an invited speaker abroad and in the media.

She has published many psychology books for professionals and for general readers and is the president and director of Académie Impact, a publishing and training company in Quebec.

Index